RENEWALS 691-4574
DATE DUE

MAY 12			
APR 30			

Demco, Inc. 38-293

D1417605

Off-Air Videotaping
in Education

Off-Air Videotaping in Education

COPYRIGHT ISSUES, DECISIONS, IMPLICATIONS

Esther R. Sinofsky

R. R. BOWKER COMPANY
New York and London, 1984

In memory of my grandmother, Channa Block,
who encouraged me in this endeavor
but did not see its conclusion.

R. R. Bowker Company
205 East Forty-Second Street, New York, NY 10017
Copyright © 1984 by Xerox Corporation
Printed and bound in the United States of America

Library of Congress Cataloging in Publication Data
Sinofsky, Esther Rita.
  Off-air videotaping in education.

  Bibliography: p.
  Includes index.
  1. Video recordings – Fair use (Copyright) – United
States.   2. Video tapes in education – Law and legislation
– United States.   I. Title.
KF3030.4.S56   1984   346.7304'82   84-18396
ISBN 0-8352-1755-8   347.306482

CONTENTS

APPENDIXES

CHAPTER REFERENCES AND BIBLIOGRAPHY   137

INDEX   157

PREFACE

*"I can make a copy for my class,
can't I? Isn't it fair use?"*

*"There's a good series on Channel . . . this semester.
Can't we tape it for our department?"*

"Aren't we covered by the fair use guidelines?"

"Didn't the Betamax *decision settle the issue?"*

Sounds familiar? Experience a sense of déjà vu? But the *real* question is: How *do you* answer these questions? Do you really know what fair use is or do you confuse it with educational use? Do you know that not all producers have endorsed the fair use guidelines for off-air videotaping? Do you really know what is meant by *copyright*? What *are* the issues? Who is right?

While this book does *not* replace legal counsel on any issue, it is meant to serve media specialists, educators, administrators, librarians, producers, distributors, and other concerned parties as a resource for charting a course through the sometimes treacherous waters known as copyright.

This book grew out of my doctoral dissertation which was an attempt to *objectively* (1) present the legal principles involved in off-air taping; (2) identify the trends and issues affecting the use of off-air taping by educational institutions; and (3) identify alternate approaches for reconciling the points of debate. Though the focus is on off-air taping, much of the information is equally valid for other media such as print and computer software.

For research purposes, it was assumed that statutory law is only valid until amended, abrogated, superseded, or invalidated by subsequent legislation or decision by the courts. Law is a slowly changing institution, not a constant, fixed tradition. The scope of the research was delimited to the off-air videotaping aspect of the copyright-reprography issue. Research and data related to other media reprography (e.g., photocopying of printed materials) was excluded unless deemed pertinent to the issue at hand. While it is believed that no leading case was omitted, not all cases that may have been related to the topic in one manner or another were included. The relevance of any court decision almost certainly depended upon my interpretation. But, even the interpretations by legal and educational experts sometimes conflicted as to the meaning and significance of a particular case.

A special thank you goes to my parents, Boris and Faye, for keeping me supplied with diet soda during the writing of the dissertation and its revision into book form; my sisters, Mindy and Aviva, for keeping the television, radio, and stereo to a low roar while I wrote; my friends and professors, for nagging me to "finish it already"; and my dog, Tara, for keeping me company during those late night/early morning writing sessions.

INTRODUCTION

Copyright law is not the creation of a given moment; rather, it is an evolutionary process reflecting attempts at accommodating disparate notions. The current Act has been depicted as bearing

> the fingerprints, footprints and scuff marks of rival pressure groups, each anxious to shape the law in its own image and likeness. Amendatory language overlays amendatory language. The singleness of purpose and the clarity of text so essential for the construction and interpretation of statutes – and absolutely vital in the exegesis of ground-breaking legislation lie buried under layers of verbiage. (A. S. Katz, 1977, pp. 172–173)

Katz further characterized the Act as "one huge legal *tell*" where "archaeologists may well fare better than jurists and lawyers in unearthing its hidden meanings" (p. 173).

The "archaeological expedition" that follows begins with a historical overview to serve as a general frame of reference. Next, it looks at the issues from the perspective of the concerned parties. Then the key issue of public access versus economics is explored, followed by a look at the fair use doctrine itself. It is impossible to investigate fair use without scrutinizing the court cases themselves for "the line which must be drawn between fair use and copyright infringement depends on an examination of the facts in each case. It cannot be determined by resort to any arbitrary rules of fixed criteria" (*Meeropol* v. *Nizer*, 1977, p. 278). Similarly in *Karll* v. *Curtis Publishing Co.* (1941), the court reasserted: "What is or is not fair use depends upon the circumstances of each particular case" (p. 51). Furthermore, according to Wasserstrom (1956):

> The United States Copyright Code, as is well known to those who have studied it and have had to apply its provisions, is, unfortunately, anything but a paradigm of careful legislative draftsmanship ... the Code contains not only broad and indefinite so-called container-terms ... but also considerable ambiguous, loose and textually inconsistent language. That being so, it has devolved upon the courts, incident to their search for, and effectuation of, legislative meaning and purpose, to fill these containers with appropriate content and reasonably to clarify, tighten and harmonize that language. (pp. 381–382)

Thus, a section is devoted to what the courts have had to say about fair use. Finally, suggested solutions to the off-air videotape recording controversy are examined, with special attention paid to the 1981 guidelines.

As it is impossible to completely "excavate" an area where judges described cases as calling "not for the judgment of Solomon but for the dexterity of Houdini" (*Fortnightly Corporation* v. *United Artists Television*, 1968, p. 6), the discussion that follows does not seek to include all the media and issues involved in the copyright–reprography controversy. Thus, for a discussion of videodiscs, for example, see Troost (1979b) in "Books, Articles, and Legislative Materials" in the section "Chapter References and Bibliography"; cable television (CATV), see *Current developments in CATV* (1981), Marke (1977), Meyers (1977), Puffer (1981), Samuels (1980), Tseng (1979); the international scene, see Arié (1980), Bloom (1980), Duemmler (1981), Keyes (1980), Klaver (1976), Minami (1980), Oekonomidis (1980), Wallace (1971); moral rights, see Strauss (1959/1963), Streibich (1975, 1976); obscenity, see *Mitchell Brothers Film Group* v. *Cinema Adult Theater* (1976, 1979); and, videocassette sales of films, see Beard (1979–80), Diamond (1975), "Does the showing ... " (1982).

1

HOW DID WE GET HERE?

As the world becomes a more complex place in which to live, the laws that regulate our society also increase in intricacy. No longer are ten commandments enough. Of the myriad regulations with which educational institutions must now cope, copyright poses some of the toughest problems because the law itself is often vague or ambiguous regarding educational situations. Even with the various negotiated guidelines on educational uses and a multitude of publications on copyright, those of us who are media specialists, educators, administrators, and librarians still frequently find ourselves asking: "Can I allow this to be done? Is it an infringement?" In answering our own questions, we find ourselves torn between the perceived educational needs of our students and the need for protection of copyright owners.

How did we get here? How did the dilemma arise? What influences are at work? This chapter explores these issues by looking first at an historical overview of copyright development, then at the problems involved with the 1976 Copyright Act, and finally at the nature of the off-air videotaping problem itself.

A HISTORICAL OVERVIEW

European Roots

The most famous medieval (circa A.D. 567) copyright case involves the manuscript entitled *Cathac*, "the fighter." St. Columba wanted to copy Abbot Finnian's *Psalter* but was refused permis-

1

sion. Clandestinely, he began copying it, but Finnian discovered this and claimed that a copy made without permission belonged to the owner of the original much like an offspring. St. Columba refused to return the copy, so the issue was taken to King Diarmid at Tara. His famous verdict was: "To every cow her calf, and consequently to every book its copy." St. Columba, however, refused to comply with the verdict. This led to the civil war deposing Diarmid; hence the manuscript's name. While the subsequent evolution of copyright law (see Table 1 for highlights) did not topple kingdoms, it did at times play a role in the political intrigues of the day. For example, in sixteenth- and seventeenth-century England, copyright was used as a means of stifling heresy by a self-censorship of the printing trade.

Renaissance Italy is usually considered the birthplace of copyright law. Originally, the granting of exclusive rights to authors and inventors by the Italian city-states took the form of patents. However, regardless of this seemingly pro-author bent, printing monopolies were granted primarily to encourage the new science of printing and not necessarily authorship. Copyright as a printing protection, rather than as an authorship protection, was echoed in the early English development of the institution. Throughout the sixteenth and seventeenth centuries, copyright belonged to the printer. An author sold his or her manuscript to a publisher for very little remuneration. The publisher received the "copy right" through its Stationers' Company membership. To survive, an author needed a patron who would provide financial support in return for a dedication of the next work.

The eighteenth century brought the first changes in this pattern. The Statute of Anne (1710), the basis of modern copyright law, vested copyright in the author, not the publisher. This decision stemmed from the publishers' appeals to Parliament to restore copyright because authors would not write without the benefit of protection. The publishers used this approach to generate greater sympathy for a new law but did not foresee a change in the old practices. Change did occur, however. Protection for publishers became protection for authors. And reconciling the interests of publishers, author, and user remains a part of the copyright dilemma even today.

The U.S. Experience

The first U.S. copyright law appeared in May 1672, when the General Court for Elections of the Massachusetts Bay Colony issued an order for John Usher. That order met all but one modern

TABLE 1   COPYRIGHT : HISTORICAL HIGHLIGHTS

Renaissance Italy	
1421	Filippo Brunelleschi, architect of the Florence cathedral dome, awarded patent for improved design of shallow-draft boats. (His design was a failure: the boat sank!)
1469	John of Speyer receives five-year monopoly for printing and selling.
1486	Marc Antonio Sabellico granted first known author's copyright for a specific title: *Decades rerum Venetarum (Decades of Venetian Affairs)*.
1491–1492	Petrus Franciscus de Ravenna receives copyright for *Foenix*.
Sixteenth- and Seventeenth-Century England	
1518 on	Royal grants for exclusive printing privileges and patents.
1534	Act of Supremacy (official licensing as a means of general censorship stemmed from Henry VIII's desire to suppress religious dissent); enforcement proved difficult.
May 4, 1557	Stationers' Company chartered by Queen Mary Tudor. (Company granted a monopoly on printing as long as it ensured nothing offensive to the Crown was printed.)
June 23, 1586	Star Chamber decree. (Partnership of Stationers' Company and government further articulated under Elizabeth I.)
Eighteenth-Century England	
1695	Stationers' Company charter expires. Commercial plagiarism wars begin.
April 10, 1710	Statute of Anne passed by Parliament. (Ends plagiarism wars.)
1735	*The Engravers' Act*, or "Hogarth's Act," passed. (The first visual copyright law.)
1769	*Millar* v. *Taylor*. (Decision: author retains a perpetual common law right in a work.)
1774	*Donaldson* v. *Beckett*. (Decision, on appeal to House of Lords: once a work is published, the perpetual common law right is replaced by the Statute of Anne.)

test for copyright protection: there was no definition of the protection time period. This oversight was corrected in 1673, when Usher again appealed to the court. In light of the Puritan respect for reading and education, it was not surprising that Massachusetts was the scene of these first laws.

Once the 13 British colonies in America gained independence, there arose a need for copyright laws, as the Statute of Anne no longer applied. In January 1783, Connecticut passed the first

"American" copyright law. March and April 1783 saw Massachusetts and Maryland pass similar laws. By May of that year, the Continental Congress had passed a resolution urging the rest of the states to pass copyright laws and even suggested features to incorporate. All states, except Delaware, passed such laws, with the Statute of Anne serving as the model for most of them. However, variations in state laws made interstate litigation difficult. In fact, it was this type of difficulty that pushed Congress to revise the Articles of Confederation in favor of the Constitution and a strong federal government. Charles C. Pinckney was responsible for the patent and copyright clause in the U.S. Constitution (Article I, Section 8, Clause 8). Thus, copyright became one of the enumerated powers.

On May 31, 1790, the first federal copyright law under the Constitution was passed by the second session of Congress. It was entitled "An Act for the Encouragement of Learning, by Securing Copies of Maps, Charts, and Books to the Authors and Proprietors of Such Copies, during the Times Therein Mentioned." A total of four general revisions of the law have taken place over the years—in 1831, 1870, 1909, and 1976. In turn, each of these revisions has been amended to accommodate new demands as changes in economics, society, and literary and artistic outlooks have occurred. Like their English confreres, U.S. writers began to see themselves as professionals; the result was a changed view of literary ownership.

As in England 60 years earlier, the question of whether a perpetual common law copyright existed independently of the statutory grant also arose in America. In *Wheaton* v. *Peters* (1834), the U.S. Supreme Court determined that there was no U.S. common law in respect to copyright, although the Court indicated that it may exist at the state level. (The 1976 Act incorporated common law protection of unpublished works, thus giving such works federal protection.) The decision reviewed the British opinions in *Millar* v. *Taylor* (1769) and *Donaldson* v. *Beckett* (1774) but added a careful observance of the minutiae of copyright compliance, to the extent that some copyrights were forfeited, an attitude that remained until recently.

From roughly 1785 to 1850, an idea developed that the question of infringement was not necessarily restricted to a quantitative measure but might involve a qualitative judgment about the importance of the appropriated part—an idea that remained a part of copyright law in the concept of fair use. Justice Joseph Story was the chief U.S. reinterpreter of English copyright doctrine between

1839 and 1845. (Despite independence and other Anglo–American conflicts, England was still looked upon as the literary center and source of custom for the United States during most of the nineteenth century.) According to Story, authors remained free to rework old materials as long as they did so in their own distinctive way. New works using substantial portions of old works were infringements. Story is perhaps best remembered for his decision in *Folsom* v. *Marsh* (1841), which established the basic criteria for fair use arguments in the U.S. courts until their incorporation into Section 107 of the 1976 Copyright Act. The decision, however, never actually mentioned fair use.

The 1909 Act was the basic copyright law until the passage of the new Act in 1976. The 1909 Act made it compulsory to have licenses for mechanical reproductions of musical works and established the American Society of Composers, Authors and Publishers (ASCAP) to collect and distribute royalty fees. It extended copyright to include novelization, adaptation, arrangement, and the like. By 1912, motion pictures had also been included. Nevertheless, the 1909 Act needed revision in order (1) to simplify and clarify the law; (2) to accommodate technological changes; and, (3) to lengthen the duration so as to conform with other countries.

As pressure began building to revise the 1909 Act – especially as radio, television, photocopying, and other technologies developed – attempts to incorporate fair use provisions in the proposed legislation grew. For example, as early as 1924, a mere 15 years after the Act's passage, the Dallinger Bill proposed a fair use exemption. Other pre–World War II attempts to incorporate fair use included the Vestal Bill and its Senate companion, the Herbert Bill (both 1931); the Sirovich bills and the Dill Bill (all 1932); and the Shotwell Committee/Thomas Bill (1940).

With no revision forthcoming, no provision for fair use made, and photocopying, especially in libraries, beginning to grow, the National Association of Book Publishers, the Joint Committee on Materials for Research of the American Council of Learned Societies, and the Social Science Research Council reached a private arrangement on the single reproduction of copyrighted manuscripts. This became known as the Gentlemen's Agreement of 1935. The concerned parties agreed that (1) hand copying had always been a student option; (2) mechanical reproductions were presumed to replace hand transcription and were governed by the same principles; and (3) the courts recognized book quotations as fair use. Therefore, the Gentlemen's Agreement provided that a single photocopy for research purposes could be made and delivered as long as the institution made no profit. Unfortunately, the agreement lacked the force of law; the organizations went out of existence leaving no successors; and the proliferation of copy machines was not foreseen. It may have served as the precursor, however, for later attempts to have concerned parties work out their own fair use guidelines for photocopying books, periodicals, and music, as well as off-air videotaping.

After World War II copyright revision did not receive serious attention until 1955, when Congress funded a series of research studies – eventually totaling 35 monographs – under the auspices of the Copyright Office. Based on the research generated, the first revision legislation was introduced in the 88th Congress on July 20, 1964. But not until 1976 would Congress finally pass a new copyright act.

In 1967 the House passed its revision bill, but the Senate's proposed legislation was not acted upon due to the cable television (CATV) issue (which was resolved in the 1976 Act). There was a period of inaction until September 9, 1974, when the Senate passed, by a vote of 70 to 1, S. 1361. Unfortunately, it was too late for House consideration that session. In the meantime, the 1971 Sound Recording Amendment extended protection to sound recordings, which had been denied copyright protection on the basis of *White-Smith Music Publishing Co.* v. *Apollo Co.* (1908). Tape piracy had grown rapidly during the 1960s, and thus Congress had been forced to act.

Finally, in 1976, Senator John L. McClellan (D-Ark.) introduced copyright revision bill S. 22, which passed 97 to 0 on February 19, 1976. On September 22, 1976, the House passed a revision bill also. However, due to differences between the two bills, a conference committee was called. The Conference Report was adopted by both houses on September 30. On October 19, 1976, President Ford signed into law PL 94-553 (90 Stat. 2541), which took effect January 1, 1978. It had taken 21 years from the 1955 congressional funding to accomplish this latest copyright law revision.

EDUCATION, COPYRIGHT, AND TECHNOLOGY

Article I, Section 8, Clause 8 of the U.S. Constitution empowers Congress to legislate copyright laws: "To promote the progress of science and useful arts, by securing for limited times to authors and inventors the exclusive right to their respective writings and discoveries." The underlying premise for the formulation of this constitutional provision was that copyright law would help shape the culture of U.S. society by providing the protection needed as an incentive for the creation and dissemination of works that would constitute the repository of our ideas, values, attitudes, beliefs, and knowledge.

At first glance, such an objective seems to echo the aim of education: "To connect man with man, to connect the present with the past, and to advance the thinking of the race" (Hutchins, 1936, p. 71). However, the continuous publication of materials to help educators and librarians cope with the copyright law in all its complexity* indicates that there are problems in applying the copyright law to educational situations. The problems reflect three interacting strands: changes in education wrought by the new technologies; gaps in the copyright law itself; and strains the new technologies place upon the copyright law.

Education and Technology

Education has been one of the professions affected by modern technology. Technology has given today's educators a wide range of instructional materials with which to work. However, the same technology has also given them the ability to reproduce, store, and transmit those materials.

Education and technology are related in two ways. On the one hand, educators have used technology to improve instruction; on the other, they have used it to cope with the growing demands a changing society has placed upon them.

Educators have continuously been involved in speculation on and experimentation with media for educational purposes. Burgeoning technologies have enhanced instruction with a dazzling array of options not available from traditional methods, that is, physically present "real time" classes and books, offering a means for a more interesting presentation of material, for individualizing studies, for including information the printed or spoken word cannot convey, and for freeing instruction from space and time limitations.

However, educators have also been pressured to meet society's changing needs. The constantly increasing demand for knowledge has correspondingly created an increased need to use copyrighted works in the schools. From the educator's view, this means a need for open access to a wide variety of materials: books, periodicals,

*For example, Association for Educational Communications & Technology, 1977a, 1977b; American Library Association, 1977; Johnston, 1978; J. K. Miller, 1975, 1979, 1981; Treece, 1977.

audio recordings, telecasts. Individualized instruction multiplies this need because each student requires different resources.

The new, inexpensive duplication methods available for almost all media have made it easier for educators to expose students to more experiences. As Kaplan (1967) pointed out:

> If man has any "natural" rights, not the least must be the right to imitate his fellows, and thus to reap where he has not sown. Education, after all, proceeds from a kind of mimicry, and "progress," if it is not entirely an illusion, depends on generous indulgence of copying. (p. 2)

These copying devices have helped instructors meet the challenge of presenting the most timely and informative lessons possible by filling in gaps caused by unavailability, which in turn is due to production time lags. They have also allowed for greater specialization of course content. At the same time, however, they have increased the educator's responsibility to media producers, especially in terms of supporting the latter's protection under copyright law.

The new emphasis on multimedia in schools and libraries has created a nonprint material duplication phenomenon that has become the center of the latest skirmish between educational institutions and producers. Those favoring classroom copying, in support of their stance, have pointed to the educational value of the programs, the ability to synchronize the viewing and study of the show, the difficulty in obtaining permission for copying, and the study guides distributed to educators for teaching a show in class. They have also pointed to the legal limbo surrounding the issue, expressing a "safety in numbers" view. Classroom copying has been differentiated from library and performance copying, the argument being that the exposure of copyrighted works in the classroom will increase the market. Those opposing such practices have pointed out that most of the literature has regarded off-air videotape recording as illegal without permission because fair use does not include copying a whole work, markets have not expanded, licensing difficulties can be surmounted, and the potential for abuse of such rights is tremendous. They have also noted that illegal videotaping has given students a bad example, that is to say, there are moral and ethical considerations involved as well.

The first videotape recorders within school price range were introduced in the mid-1960s. By the 1970s, whole tape libraries were being developed. The first to oppose the building of such libraries via off-air taping was the Columbia Broadcasting System (CBS). In 1973, CBS sued Vanderbilt University for videotaping TV news programs, editing the tapes, and making copies for use by scholars; Vanderbilt countersued for abridgement of academic freedom. These suits were dismissed without prejudice in 1976 as Section 108 (f) (3) of the new Copyright Act (see Appendix A) included a subsection permitting the videotaping of commercial TV news programs. However, documentaries, magazine-format, and other public affairs broadcasts of general interest were not covered by the "Vanderbilt exemption," as the section came to be called. Also excluded were the multitude of other TV programs such as sit coms, soap operas, game shows, and talk shows.

Not only did the new Act fail to delineate off-air videotaping boundaries for various TV shows, but the legislative history (H.R. 94-1476; H.R. 94-1733; S. 94-473) failed as well. The congressional committee recommended that, as with print and music guidelines, educators and producers work out guidelines and then submit them to the committee for consideration and incorporation into the legislative history. Thus, educators and producers returned to their respective sides of the fence, and the stalemate continued until October 1981, when guidelines for off-air videotaping for educational uses were announced.

Gaps in the Copyright Law

The ink had barely dried on the newest *General Revision of Copyright Law* (U.S. Congress, 1976) when criticisms and predictions of revision began to appear. The law that will probably be the basis for authorship and dissemination for the last quarter of this century was described as vague and ambiguous and as leaving gaps with no clear solutions. It was faulted for being corpulent and raising almost as many problems as it solved. A. E. Katz (1977) asserted that it "may very well not have the promised flexibility, nor solve the problems which gave rise to its enactment in the first place" (p. 214). Parris (1977) called it an act "born of exhaustion following more than twenty years of serious congressional considerations" (p. 564).

Henn (1978) criticized the new law for being unduly lengthy, detailed, and complicated. He prophesied annual amendment proposals, some of which would be enacted, until the 1976 Act collapsed under its own weight, before the year 2000. While these predictions may sound slightly farfetched—the present revision took 20 years to legislate and came nearly 70 years after the last revision—they are partly sustained by the fact that several bills that would amend the Copyright Act with regard to home off-air taping are under consideration by the House Committee on the Judiciary. The first such bill was introduced October 20, 1981, one day after the Ninth Circuit's reversal of the *Universal City Studios, Inc.* v. *Sony Corporation of America* (hereinafter *Sony*) decision and six days after the educational off-air guidelines were read into the *Congressional Record*. Like Henn, Barbara Ringer (1977b), the former U.S. Register of Copyrights, commented on the continuous revision process that is copyright law: "However tired Congress may be of the intricacies of copyright law and the importunings of copyright lobbyists, it has probably not seen the end of copyright revision in this decade" (pp. 976–977). The unresolved issues in copyright seem to revolve around the interpretation of fair use, educational uses, and the changing role of libraries and information networks.

Congress itself built a need for revision into the Act. For example, the 1976 Act did not resolve the issue of computer software copyrightability. The National Commission on New Technological Uses of Copyrighted Works (CONTU) was charged with the task of deciding what protection, if any, to grant computer programs. It issued its final report on July 31, 1978. The Computer Software Copyright Act (PL 96-517, 94 Stat. 3015), which amended Sections 101 and 117 of the 1976 Act, passed both houses in November 1980 and was signed into law by President Carter on December 12, 1980. But even this act has left certain areas unclear.

There has been general agreement among legislators, judges, and commentators that "the issue of fair use . . . is the most troublesome in the whole law of copyright" (*Dellar* v. *Samuel Goldwyn, Inc.*, 1939, p. 165). In fact, fair use is a contradiction of the basic concept of copyright: Copyright grants an author an exclusive monopoly on a particular work; fair use provides that someone other than the author can have certain rights regarding the work—and have those rights without payment to or notification of the copyright owner. Is it any wonder, then, that controversy surrounds fair use?

In an attempt to rectify this problem, the new Act included Section 107 (see Appendix B), which expressed the now famous four criteria of fair use:

1. the purpose and character of the use, including whether such use is of a commercial nature or is for nonprofit educational purposes;

2. the nature of the copyrighted work;
3. the amount and substantiality of the portion used in relation to the copyrighted work as a whole; and
4. the effect of the use upon the potential market for or value of the copyrighted work.

Unfortunately, however, no actual definition of fair use was included with these criteria, nor was there an indication of their priority with respect to application. Furthermore, by including teaching, scholarship, and research along with the universally acknowledged fair use instances of criticism, comment, and news reporting, distinctions between fair use and exempted use were blurred. In addition, the fair use sections are so occupied with the photocopying issue that new technologies were not given any meaningful direction. All these compounded the problem of fair use interpretation.

Probably one of the most serious problems in fair use interpretation – even with the negotiated guidelines – is educational off-air videotaping of TV broadcasts. Expressly left unresolved by Congress and thus very much undefined, it quickly became a hotly debated topic. The key questions for both educational and home off-air videotaping are Where do the copyright owner's rights end and those of the user begin? How are the public's interests defined in light of those of the copyright owner?

Although included in Section 101 definitions, videotapes are not further considered in the new Act except in the subsections of Sections 108 and 111. In other words, as the new copyright law did not set down clear guidelines of off-air videotaping, the dissemination and transfer of information versus the protection of copyright owner's rights – two areas of vital concern to instructional technologists, librarians, authors, producers, judges, and other parties – have remained in conflict despite the recent attempt by Congress to harmonize them.

Copyright and the New Technologies

Orwell's *1984* has been read as a "warning that the values on which our culture is based – of individualism, idealism, and free expression – are in the most immediate possible danger, not from any particular ideology or political system, but simply from the juggernaut of technology" (Ringer, 1976, p. 300). On the one hand, in today's information-oriented culture, technology has provided decision making with improved tools and presented new frontiers to challenge the intellect. The medium is the message – and something more. Television, radio, computers, and other media that play such an important role in our daily lives "are generating fresh interactions and new permutations. . . . [They] are obliging the practitioners of creative and interpretative skills to rethink their own relationships and to ponder new ones" (Taubman cited in Krasilvosky, 1969, p. 413). On the other hand, as new technologies are developed and adopted, they affect the economic, political, and social strands of our society.

The copyright dilemma caused by the new technologies is not a recent phenomenon. For example, the first U.S. copyright act was passed in 1790 and amended in 1802 to include prints; the 1909 Act had extended copyright protection to motion pictures by 1912, but sound recordings were not included until 1972. The inability of copyright law easily to accommodate the "graphic revolution," that is, the contemporary "ability to make, preserve, and transmit . . . precise images" (Boorstin, 1964, p. 12) has been called the Laocöon shortfall (S. Timberg, 1980, p. 317). Despite this problem, users and owners alike still see copyright law as almost "the only public policy that is concerned with the relationships among the new neopublishing technologies, intellectual creativity, intellectual property, and the paramount social value of promoting 'the Progress of Science and useful Art' " (Henry, 1975, 2:2).

The creation and dissemination of intellectual property have become increasingly important and complex, for the technological revolution's relentless reshaping and expansion of available and efficient methods of communication have resulted in the formation of new groups that challenge the traditional exclusive rights of authors under copyright protection. The major feature of the "reprographic revolution," of course, is the ability to produce single copies economically. These copies are produced by the same technologies that have made massive data bases and unique educational materials possible. In other words, copying devices have become a concern because they provide not only important services but the means to duplicate those services at will, without permission of the services' owners.

Exploring the issue of new technology and the copyright law, a 1968 UCLA project decided that new technology may result – and has already resulted – in a clash between U.S. copyright theory's dual values of private reward and public benefit. In a postscript to his *Williams & Wilkins Company* v. *United States* (1972) decision, Commissioner Davis commented:

> The issues raised by this case are but part of a larger problem which continues to plague our institutions with ever-increasing complex-

ity—how best to reconcile, on the one hand, the rights of authors and publishers under the copyright laws with, on the other hand, the technological improvements in copying techniques and the legitimate public need for rapid dissemination of scientific and technical literature. The conflict is real; the solution not simple. (p. 686)

Professor Nimmer (1968), the renowned copyright authority, reflected a similar view of the technological impact upon the copyright law.

Ultimately, the clash may not mean sacrificing either one of the values; rather, it may mean learning to accommodate these values in a technological era. Ease of duplication is now a part of our technological ability. Video- and audiorecorders, computers, and photocopiers will not simply disappear. It would appear that as long as technology continues to replace older practices, copyright problems will remain.

NATURE OF THE PROBLEM

In a 1975 lecture, Leonard Feist (cited in Streibich, 1975), then executive vice-president of the National Music Publishers Association, noted: "In our contemporary society, plagiarism is a crime upon which society frowns. Copyright infringement, however, is something like speeding. It's considered by many to be quite all right as long as you don't get caught" (p. 7). For example, prior to the enactment of the 1976 Copyright Law, many school districts—to protect themselves legally—made regulations forbidding off-air taping, yet their personnel continued to videotape (Troost, 1978b).

There is little statistical data available regarding the actual number of teachers and students involved in the use of televised instruction. Robert Gold has testified (*Hearings*, 1979),* with respect to WNET (New York), WGBH (Boston), and KCET (Los Angeles), the three Public Broadcasting Service (PBS) stations responsible for most of the service's programming production: "This past year close to 40 percent of WNET's total broadcast week was devoted to children's programming, including 35 hours each week of in-school classroom courses which reached approximately 650,000 students in 1,700 schools" (p. 56). In addition, there were college credit courses. At the same hearings, Eric Smith, counsel for PBS, quoted (but did not name) a 1976–1977 study by the Corporation for Public Broadcasting and the National Center for Educational Statistics. The study estimated that 2,275,000 teachers

---

*U.S., Congress, House, Committee on the Judiciary, *Off-air taping for educational use.*

and 46 million students fell within the study's ambit. Of these, 950,000 teachers used TV; of the 20 million students who used TV, 15 million received a regular portion of their instruction via TV during the year of the study.

> This same study further provided some insight into the use of television programs in schools through off-air recording. Of the 90,000 school buildings encompassed within the study, 63,500 had television programming available through all sources including off-air recording.
>
> Of these, an estimated 25,000 buildings contain at least one videotape recorder; and in 80 percent of these buildings, off-the-air taping was done.
>
> This would represent over 500,000 teachers, teaching almost 11 million students with television programs taped off the air. (*Hearings*, 1979, p. 50)

The question arises: Did the TV programs used by over 500,000 teachers to teach almost 11 million students involve the legal or illegal use of copyrighted material? According to the Association of Media Producers (AMP), many educators still mistakenly believe their not-for-profit status allows them to copy legally without authorization; those with some copyright knowledge claim fair use privileges. As far as the AMP is concerned, copying an entire motion picture or telecast without the owner's permission is a violation of the copyright law. (The AMP did not accept the off-air guidelines of October 19, 1981, as will be discussed in Chapter 4.)

In a similar vein, others claimed that it is illegal to videotape programs off the air and asserted that making a copy of an entire copyrighted work is never fair use. Thus, since most instructors do not do the actual taping themselves but request this as a service from the school's media centers, media professionals are caught between requests from teachers and prohibitions from media producers.

However, assertions such as those made by the AMP as to what constitutes illegal duplication are not completely accurate. With the newest revision of the Copyright Act (1976), an agreement was reached on guidelines for classroom photocopying of books and periodicals. This agreement defined Section 107 – the "fair use" section – of the new Act as it affected print duplication. (A similar one was reached for educational uses of music.) But the section was not immediately explicated for off-air taping. The House Committee on the Judiciary report on the 1976 Copyright Law (H. Rept.

94-1476) observed: "The problem of off-the-air taping for nonprofit classroom use of copyrighted audiovisual works incorporated in radio and television broadcasts has proved to be difficult to resolve" (p. 71). It went on to say that fair use "has some limited application in this area" (p. 71) but needed further exploration in order to establish guidelines to which the concerned parties would agree.

Negotiated guidelines for educational off-air taping were finally announced five years later, in October 1981. However, the guidelines were not adopted by all the producers and did not end the controversy over off-air taping. The *Sony* (1979, 1981) case was appealed to the Supreme Court, which handed down its decision in January 1984. Its possible effect on educational taping remains unclear. In conjunction with the *Sony* appeal, several bills were proposed in Congress to settle the home off-air taping tangle. Some of the proposals would exempt at-home taping; others would impose on the manufacturers a value-added tax for royalties on equipment and blank tapes. How the guidelines would be affected, if at all, is unclear.

To further complicate matters, Section 108, which deals with library photocopying, came up for its five-year scrutiny. The King Research report (*Libraries, Publishers and Photocopying*), conducted for the Copyright Office's Section 108 status report, was published in May 1982. This brought the photocopying issue back to life as publishers claimed they had been too liberal in their earlier photocopying permissions and sought to renegotiate the terms. Through the Association of American Publishers (AAP), publishers began a series of litigations to check corporate photocopying of scientific and technical journals and to keep academia within fair-use photocopying guidelines for classroom use of print materials.*

The Register of Copyright's report (U.S. Copyright Office, 1983) to Congress on implementation of Section 108 included both statutory and nonstatutory recommendations. Among the nonstatutory ones were congressional encouragement of participation in existing collective licensing arrangements and development of voluntary guidelines by concerned parties. In addition, two studies for the next five-year report were recommended. One would explore a surcharge on equipment; the other, various copyright compensation systems based on a percentage of photocopying. As

---

*The corporations were American Cyanamid Co. and E. R. Squibb & Sons; New York University was the academic institution involved. All suits were settled out of court.

Section 107 guidelines are open to future changes, the question arises whether possible revisions of Section 108 will have any impact on them.

These conflicting demands and legal opinions have resulted in "media professionals and administrative school employees . . . being asked to function as attorneys, when even attorneys themselves cannot agree as to what is correct" (Gerletti cited in *Hearings*, 1979, p. 165). Cardozo (1976–1977) asked: "What shall I tell my client?" (p. 59). But he failed to find an answer because of the Act's uncertainties. Troost (1979a) illustrated this point with letters from two lawyers.* One advised his client school district that off-air taping of commercially broadcast TV was not fair use under the 1976 Act. The attorney recommended that district personnel desist from further unauthorized taping, erase all illegally retained materials, and adopt a policy consistent with the 1976 Act. In contrast, the other attorney advised his school district that it was acceptable to tape shows unavailable for rental and to retain them until a preview copy could be procured or they were erased for lack of interest. He did caution, however, that this did not cover wholesale copying and that limits had to be set on time, content, and use of the copyrighted works.

In copyright infringements cases, the teacher, librarian, and even the school district may be sued. Under the legal concept of constructive knowledge, an "ignorance of the law excuses no man" approach, the copyright defendant would still be liable, only the remedies available would be affected. Yet, as Chafee (1945a) remarked: "To require officials, judges and lawyers to work with a statute which is intricate and leaves many important points unsettled is like asking an engineer to do his calculations with a warped and illegible slide rule" (p. 514). Clearly, the person in charge of audio-visual operations requires concise, accurate information to bridge the gap between desirable practice and legal definition. While further legislative and judicial interpretations of copyright and off-air taping are needed, there are areas that can and, indeed, should be analyzed for the benefit of instructors and administrators who daily deal with off-air taping. Some of these are explored in the remaining chapters.

SUMMARY

Although ancient forms of copyright existed, it is actually the product of the Gutenberg era. Copyright was originally designed

---

*The example cited here occurred prior to the development of guidelines, but does highlight the type of problem that plagued media specialists.

to protect the infant printing trade. It then became a tool of censorship and press control; it also gave the members of the Stationers' Company regulatory powers and a monopoly on the book trade. To meet the needs of another era, copyright again shifted perspective, this time to protect authors. However, instead of continuing to change according to the needs of the time, copyright seems to have frozen on the idea of authors' rights. A dilemma then developed on how best to reconcile author, publisher, and public interests in copyrighted works. This dilemma remains to the present time.

Three interacting factors characterize the problems of applying copyright law to educational situations. One factor is the changes in education wrought by the new technologies. Educators have used technology for the twofold purpose of improving instruction and coping with the growing demands of a changing society. But the technology that has made this possible has also made duplication of copyrighted materials as easy as pressing a button. Students' needs are pitted against those of copyright owners. Another factor arises from gaps in the copyright law itself. The 1976 Copyright Act is the first U.S. copyright act actually to include the judicial concept of fair use. However, the fair use discussion lacked specific definition and application criteria and expanded the concept's scope so as to include teaching, scholarship, and research. While finally addressing such issues as cable television, this latest revision did not clarify newer issues such as off-air taping for either educational or home use. The third factor affecting copyright law stems from the relationship between the new technologies and the law itself. New reprographic technologies have facilitated the dissemination of information in the public interest, one of copyright's goals. This has brought them into conflict with copyright's other goal—rewarding the creator.

In terms of educational off-air taping, there is a lack of statistical data on off-air videotaping practices by educational institutions. Under the current negotiated off-air taping guidelines (October 1981), this data may not be critical. However, legislative changes in the copyright law or judicial changes in its interpretation may require a better accounting of such practices. Regardless of the eventual outcome, those who deal with off-air taping decisions in educational institutions can be held liable for any infringements and therefore need to keep abreast of copyright developments.

2

THE GREAT DEBATE

What do educators and copyright proprietors consider the key issues in the educational off-air videotaping debate? Educators focus on whether copyright owners are furthering or hindering educational innovation; copyright proprietors center on the economic impact of off-air taping. Underlying both points of view is the question of using possible profits to support a worthy cause not necessarily chosen by the copyright owner. (Even the Internal Revenue Service gives us the option to contribute a dollar of our tax money to the presidential campaign fund.)

In its comparative analysis of copyright issues undertaken to aid Senator McClellan's committee, the Cambridge Research Institute (1973) concluded that educational interests wanted free access to materials and claimed that proprietors suffered little damage by such use. Furthermore, educators claimed, "Since the educational system does not have funds to buy for the students what might under their definition of fair use be freely taken, the author-publishers are not deprived of any sales of these materials for educational purposes" (p. 39). The proprietors, not unnaturally, disagreed with this economic prediction. They claimed such access to their materials would reduce already small profit margins and would destroy the incentive to produce. Furthermore, "the lack of funds that schools suffer for the purchase of materials is not a good rationale for creating an educational exemption" (Bender cited in "Symposium," 1977, p. 11).

THE COPYRIGHT PROPRIETORS

According to Aleinikoff (1980), in educational off-air taping the first and third fair use factors (a nonprofit educational purpose and copying the entire program, respectively) are set from the start. Of the remaining two factors, the second, the nature of the copyrighted work, is not significant. The fourth, then, becomes the critical key: whether or not there is a decrease in profits.

That copyright proprietors perceive off-air taping as a threat can be seen from the following sampling of opinions. A 1975 *New York Times* editorial (cited in "Symposium," 1977) declared:

> In the age of photocopying, computers, taping and broadcasting, the notion of individual creativity is all the more relevant. Well-intentioned amendments to the revision bill . . . would destroy an author's fundamental right to negotiate in the free market place. (p. 2)

Johnson (1981) charged, "The pirates of the information age do not carry cutlasses, nor do they seek gold-laden ships. Instead, they are trying to obtain and use, for free, the . . . software that consumes more and more of the . . . budget" (p. 14). Nimmer (1975) described the thrust of such economic concerns:

> One who creates a work for educational or scientific purposes may not suffer greatly by an occasional unauthorized reproduction. But if every school or library may by purchasing one or two copies of a particular work supply a demand for numerous copies through . . . [reprography], the market for educational and scientific materials would be almost completely obliterated. This could well discourage authors from creating works of an educational or scientific nature. (p. 1054)

At the 1979 congressional hearing on educational off-air videotaping, one of the forums for copyright proprietors and educators to explain their concerns, James LeMay, then of the Association of Media Producers (AMP), summarized his group's concern as follows: "In a dangerous irony, what promised to bring the classroom into the 20th century now threatens the very existence of the producers and creators who pioneered this exciting medium" (p. 20). For example, in *Encyclopaedia Britannica Educational Corporation* v. *Crooks* (1978) – more commonly known as the *BOCES* case – the Learning Corporation of America testified that in 1975 its licensing agreement with the Board of Cooperative Educational Services (BOCES) of Erie County, New York, for 16mm film purchases amounted to $12,676.25; by 1977, it had shrunk to $1,703.75.

LeMay also pointed out the danger inherent in decisions that equate the educational media industry with Hollywood, commercial TV networks, and similar enterprises. The educational media industry requires greater copyright protection vis-à-vis educational reprography because it is basically comprised of small companies. For example, in 1978, 43.2 percent of the companies had gross annual sales of $500,000 or less; 7 percent earned $5 million or more. These companies have a limited market: schools, colleges, and libraries. As a result, a limited number of copies of an audiovisual product are produced and sold. For example, a school district will purchase only one or two copies of a 16mm educational film, one filmstrip for use in several grades. A film is considered successful when a few hundred copies are sold during its lifetime; a filmstrip, when a few thousand are sold over a five- to ten-year period. The initial production investment in audio-visual materials is substantial. Churchill (1980) explained that a film produced for $20,000 must sell 285 prints merely to recoup the initial production costs. Stuart Finley (*Hearings,* 1979), of the Independent Media Producers Association, echoed this concern for small companies. He also pinpointed the duplication of preview copies as a growing hazard to the industry.

In other words, there are several factors already affecting the economic viability of the educational media industry: a substantial initial production investment, a limited market, limited sales, and an extended sales period. Duplication of educational materials without remuneration to the copyright owner severely strains the already delicate economic situation. Gilkey (1969/1972) has contended that uncontrolled duplication would reduce potential sales to a point where either the cost of the product would be greatly increased, the incentive for creation of materials would be reduced, or the producer would be forced out of business. Other economic factors that have led to a decline in the total educational media industry sales from 1974 to 1977 include cuts in funding for educational media acquisitions, reductions in the number of actual school buildings, and increases in consortia and other means of centralization.

The off-air taping policies adopted by organizations such as the Public Broadcasting Service (PBS) and Agency for Instructional Television (see Appendix C) have been criticized as having furthered off-air taping because educational institutions go beyond these authorized shows by taping and retaining commercially produced broadcasts as well. This unlicensed off-air taping, according to LeMay (*Hearings*, 1979), "has forced several commercial producers and distributors to draw back from their partnerships with both public and commercial television stations" (p. 20).

In 1979, the AMP reported a decrease in educational programming licensed by commercial producers due to decreasing revenues in nonbroadcast format resulting from unauthorized off-air taping (Callison, 1981). Mills (1976), quoting Ivan Bender, claimed unauthorized off-air taping unlawful because it deprives those with educational distribution rights to TV programs of potential income. DeFelice (1978–1979) opined that copyright owners may therefore find movie theater and prerecorded video-format marketing more profitable than TV. If so, the public could be deprived of many excellent shows currently available via standard commercial TV broadcast.

The Training Media Distributors Association (TMDA) (*Hearings*, 1979), composed mainly of small businesses, viewed so-called fair use videotaping as unauthorized copying of television broadcasts. It considered such videotaping a major erosion of badly needed copyright protection, a serious threat to its business, and an encouragement to widespread piracy. Among the 11 points enumerated by the TMDA as part of its testimony were the following:

> The "fair use" concept does not arise out of any need of educators for instructional materials from training and educational media producers which cannot be currently provided by traditional sale, rental, and licensing programs offered to educational institutions at reasonable prices.
>
> "Fair use" off-the-air copying permits the unregulated proliferation of unauthorized copies, creating an environment in which piracy will be rampant. There is no effective way to control the use of this material either within or outside of educational institutions.
>
> Unauthorized "fair use" copying could effectively deny to training media producers the protection of both civil and criminal provisions of the copyright law.
>
> Even before the "fair use" question has been resolved by Congress, certain educators are already encouraging their colleagues to "claim 'fair use' " when they do not wish to negotiate licenses for materials they want to copy. The "fair use" concept thus contributes to an abusive, lawless attitude toward copyright owners.
>
> The concept of unauthorized "fair use" off-the-air videotaping offers the risk of quickly degenerating from off-the-air copying to simply copying anything at hand. This tendency *already exists to an alarming degree.*

The goal of some "fair use" advocates is to use unauthorized copying as a means of financing educational programs at the involuntary expense of media producers. (pp. 160–161)

The TMDA also noted that unauthorized taping of training materials from TV would make it virtually impossible to license such shows for telecasting. In addition, the TMDA claimed that it was misleading to say that off-air taping involved basically network shows.

LeMay (*Hearings*, 1979) characterized government involvement in allowing off-air videotaping as dangerous to the educational media industry. First, if private producers and distributors do not receive their profits, there is no money for investment in new productions. "This is not speculation; already we have seen the first decrease in production in the history of the industry" (p. 21). This decrease is substantiated by a 1979 AMP report that indicated substantial drops in media production. The end result may be less materials to offer the educational community (Callison, 1981). (Whether this decline was the result of government involvement, off-air taping, educational cutbacks, or the general state of the economy was not clarified, however.) Second, governmental subsidizing of educational materials production could lead to a "national curriculum" and an annihilation of the private sector. This was exactly what happened in Canada, where the Ontario Educational Communications Authority almost completely eliminated the private sector.

Another governmental subsidizing issue centered on whether TV programs produced with government funds were in the public domain and therefore could be freely taped. *Schnapper* v. *Foley* (1979) seemed to have stymied the arguments that federal funding of a show granted automatic off-air taping rights. Schnapper, the editor at Public Affairs Press, brought the action against several federal agencies and their heads including William E. Foley, Barbara Ringer, and PBS. Schnapper requested an injunction that (1) invalidated copyright on a film series commissioned by the government, (2) prohibited future such copyrights, and (3) prohibited federal agency heads from contracting copyrighted works or from controlling the contents of such works. Schnapper also wanted a declaratory judgment that (1) all works produced with government funds are not copyrightable, (2) all such past, present, and future copyrights are null and void, and (3) any contract between a U.S. agency or official and a private party that gives the agency or official any control over the contents of such works is null and void.

In his decision, District Judge Smith explained that claims for injunctive relief were dismissed for lack of jurisdiction. Section 105 of the 1976 Act declared that government works are in the public domain. However, the films were made by private parties and therefore have a "private" copyright. The court found in favor of the defendants and granted their request for dismissal.

DeFelice (1978–1979), Popham (*Hearings*, 1979), and Reiner (1979) questioned whether off-air videotaping hurt the box office receipts and royalties of old shows, especially in terms of possible syndication on local stations. Reruns are important because the first-run network license fee normally does not cover production costs. (The first-run license, executed before production begins, permits two showings of each episode of a series during the year of production with a renewal option for the next four years.)

In the usual chain of payments, TV broadcasters pay TV and movie royalties for the right to show the program on TV. In turn, broadcasters are compensated by the advertisers for advertising time during the telecast. When we buy the advertised products, we, as consumers, are indirectly paying for the program. However, as many of the programs telecast by local stations are originally broadcast on network TV, it is predicted that off-air taping will reduce the local station's audience, thereby reducing revenues generated by reruns. Thus, according to Meyer (1971), *Teleprompter Corporation* v. *Columbia Broadcasting System* (1974), and *Sony* (1979), if people record and replay a program on their own systems, when a rerun is shown on TV the audience will be smaller. A smaller audience will not attract advertisers to sponsor the rerun. Lacking a sponsor, the TV station will not pay a copyright owner for a broadcast license. The copyright owner loses financially. Audience size is therefore critical since it influences the fees that advertisers pay the networks and, in turn, the fees that the networks pay the producers.

Also upsetting the balance is the videotape recorder's (VTR) editing capabilities. If advertisements are edited out of a taped show, advertisers lose potential sales. This could upset the delicate symbiosis existing among copyright owners, broadcasters, and advertisers.

DeFelice (1978–1979), Popham (*Hearings*, 1979), and Reiner (1979) also questioned the effect of unauthorized off-air taping upon the burgeoning market for prerecorded videotapes and videodiscs. Since a VTR can record and play back new programs, it has a versatility the videodisc, which merely replays prerecorded programs, and prepackaged tapes lack. The fear is that the

VTR's versatility will hinder the development of the other two formats for new motion picture markets. (The threat that videodisc technology once posed is now no longer as great, particularly for commercial applications, since many companies have either phased out or abandoned research and development in this area.)

Popham (*Hearings*, 1979) noted that local stations need protection from legal liability resulting from unauthorized uses of their programs. A related legal problem remarked upon by Donna Sessa (*Hearings*, 1979), of the American Broadcasting Companies (ABC), was that the networks are basically a vehicle for providing films and taped shows to the public. In other words, the show has been created and produced by someone else, and the networks only have the right to promote and subsequently broadcast the program. The stations simply do not have the authority to grant licensing or taping requests for such shows.

Robert Hynes (*Hearings*, 1979), of the National Broadcasting Company (NBC), observed that broadcast-only rights are true of sports programs and most entertainment shows. Thus, a TV copyright does not concern the station alone. Those involved in a program as producers and talent or with the music, graphics, scripts, and so forth may not want to permit even a so-called authorized off-air taping. For example, Ms. Sessa mentioned that her station had contracts with the Writers Guild that obligated the station to protect copyrightable literary materials and to ensure that they do not become part of the public domain.

John McGuire (*Hearings*, 1979), executive secretary of the Screen Actors Guild, explained that his organization's interest in off-air taping evolved from the payment scales for replay and supplemental markets. Actors, writers, and directors realize that the use of television programs for educational purposes may represent the finest possible use of the products they help create, but, while not opposed to fair use and off-air taping, they do not receive their appropriate fees. Furthermore, programs taped off the air for classroom use are in direct competition with those specifically made for classroom use. This means some actors are not being paid for their services and, at the same time, are reducing their colleagues' employment opportunities.

Bistline (1977) attributed the lack of guidelines to this multiparty interest. Working with print involves authors, publishers, and users; however, TV copyright affects networks, actors, producers, and directors, to name just a few.

In addition to supporting the statements of his ABC and NBC counterparts, Joe Bellon (*Hearings*, 1979), of CBS refuted fair use and free access claims based on the concept of "the public air-waves." People are under the misconception that "because television broadcasts are transmitted over the 'public airwaves,' they thereby lose some copyright protection and thus may be freely used by those who record these broadcasts off the air" (p. 43).

Two recent circuit court decisions affecting subscription televi-sion (STV), such as ON-TV, appear to support Bellon's contention that "the public airwaves" is a misconception: *Chartwell Commu-nications Group* v. *Westbrook* (1980) and *National Subscription Television* v. *S & H TV* (1981). Both STV cases dealt with the legal-ity of signal decoder boxes sold to individuals to enable them to unscramble STV signals and watch a station's programming with-out the monthly subscription charges. In *Chartwell,* Circuit Judge Brown observed, "The dual nature of STV is that while it may be available to the general public, it is intended for the exclusive use of paying subscribers. Availability and use are separate concepts" (p. 465). He also dismissed the argument that the defendants were "not assisting anyone in receiving the signals but just helping people clarify what they have already received" as "not persua-sive" (p. 466). Addressing the public airwaves argument in *Na-tional Subscription Television,* Circuit Judge Trask answered: "Although the public owns the airwaves, Congress and the FCC are charged with regulating them in the public interest. That inter-est would seemingly not be served by the demise of a product for which there is clearly considerable consumer demand" (p. 826).

THE EDUCATORS

William C. Warren (1967) once commented:

Successive ages have drawn different balances among the interest of the writer in the control and exploitation of his intellectual prop-erty, the related interest of the publisher, and the competing inter-est of society in the untrammeled dissemination of ideas.

[Kaplan's counsel] that the greater emphasis should be placed on the public's interest in the free accessibility of ideas is particularly appropriate in an era when freedom of expression is frequently under attack and when the means of dissemination of ideas are in-creasingly concentrated in fewer hands. (p. viii)

Troost (1980) expands on this:

Something that copyright proprietors are perhaps unaware of is the actual extent of access to educational information. There are wealthy educational institutions with generous funds available for the purchase of films and other television shows. Conversely, there are many institutions where any budgets for even film rental—let alone purchase—is meager or nonexistent. The prevalent economic situation points to much smaller, rather than larger, budgets for support services such as film rentals or purchases. The economic effects of off-air taping on copyright proprietors must be weighed against the degree of access to information. (p. 34)

Gus Steinhilber (*Hearings,* 1979), of the National School Boards Association and the Ad Hoc Committee on Copyright Law, a coalition of nonprofit organizations representing elementary, secondary, and higher education and public and school libraries, testified that the Ad Hoc Committee did not seek to tape everything off the air without limitation and retain it for indefinite use under the banner of fair use, but it did believe that the dissemination of information was very important. Any law interpreted as preventing the constitutionally encouraged dissemination and use of writings and discoveries was to be suspected of unconstitutionality; that is, a strict construction of the copyright law in the classroom context helps undermine the overarching constitutional concern with promoting access to knowledge (Hayes, 1978). Krasilovsky (1969) expressed concern that a lack of public support would lead to a national form of education; that is, if innovative and experimental cultural and educational uses of copyrighted works were discouraged, a mass culture and homogenized form of national education and expression would result. He therefore urged public support for some of the expense of balancing private rights and public interests. In other words, without special access to copyrighted works, educators were concerned that students would be deprived of individualized, high quality learning experiences.

According to educators, access to TV shows by teachers and students was currently limited. These limitations, they claimed, were overcome by means of educational off-air taping. Howard Hitchens (*Hearings,* 1979), then executive director of the Association for Educational Communications and Technology (AECT), referring to an unnamed study conducted by the Corporation for Public Broadcasting and the National Center for Educational Statistics in the mid-1970s, noted that a major finding was that broadcast schedules hinder the educational use of TV. For example, a good program may be aired in the wrong semester for use; students may not be able to watch a show at home because they are at work or others in the family wish to watch a different show or they cannot receive the channel. Robert Gerletti (*Hearings,* 1979), director of the Los Angeles County superintendent of school's educational media division, similarly pointed out that many valuable programs were aired at times when schools were closed or students were scheduled for other educational activities. Videotape was the technological solution for later use of these programs in classroom instruction.

In his district court decision, Judge Ferguson (*Sony,* 1979) explained:

> The purpose of . . . [noncommercial off-air taping] is to increase access to the material plaintiffs choose to broadcast. This increase in access is consistent with the First Amendment policy of providing the fullest possible access to information through the public airwaves. . . . This access is not just a matter of convenience. . . . Access has been limited not simply by inconvenience but by the basic need to work. Access to the better program has also been limited by the competitive practice of counterprogramming. (p. 682)

Like Ferguson, Clark (1979–1980) argued that off-air taping increases public access to information limited by the TV industry's counterprogramming practices. Instead of being limited to one channel at a time, the public can use the VTR to tape a second channel for later viewing. Clark also noted that the broadcasts are delivered free of charge over the public airwaves: "The purpose of the use of the VTR . . . [is] to further the public interest in the dissemination of material voluntarily broadcast" (p. 677).

Clark identified yet another limitation to access: TV broadcasts are not as readily available to viewers as are printed materials.

> Clearly we shall have to contend with network insistence on its monopoly over television imagery for the foreseeable future. How strange this is as regards the public interest can be understood by imagining that newspapers like *The New York Times,* or books and articles, were available for only a single reading—and then withdrawn by management and never seen again. (Kellner, 1980, p. 100)

Classes in film and TV study are particularly hard hit by this limitation (Mast, 1980). Nevins (1978) likened it to a literature teacher or lawyer not having a copy of the work or case in question and thus being forced to discuss the issues purely from memory. At the 1977 Airlie House Conference on Video Recording for Educational Uses, William Singer, a lawyer and president of Prime Time School

Television, which distributes information on educationally valuable TV programs to educators, echoed the concern that an in-depth analysis of a program cannot be accomplished on the basis of one showing. Rather, a copy of the work must be present to allow for a full exploration and criticism (cited in B. Timberg, 1980).

Yet another limitation to access is the notice inserted after the copyright symbol:

> All rights are reserved. Except for use in a review, reproduction or utilization of this work in whole or part in any form by an electronic, mechanical, or other means, now known or hereafter invented, including xerography and recording, or in any information storage and retrieval system, is forbidden without written permission.

Not only do such notices ignore fair use of copyrighted materials, they are purely the invention of publishers. The copyright law contains no mention of such a notice (Magarrell, 1980; Yankwich, 1954).

Judy Sessions (*Hearings*, 1979), an American Library Association member representing college libraries, complained that even if one wished to buy a prerecorded videotape of a program, the program in question is not always available for purchase or even for rental. Or, if a program is available for purchase, it often takes six months for delivery (see also Aleinikoff, 1980). Charles Adams (*Hearings*, 1979) of the Phoenix (Arizona) Union High School District similarly observed that the availability of TV programs for sale ranges from six to nine months after the telecast to never, not even for lease. Furthermore, there is no indication at the time of the original telecast whether it will be made available. The Consortium of University Film Centers (*Hearings*, 1979) added: "Many important teaching moments are currently lost because a program may be so timely that it will never be released for classroom use" (p. 159; see also Herring, 1980). In other words, users avail themselves of reprography not in order to avoid payment but rather to fill an immediate need.

A related issue was the difficulty in obtaining a license for off-air videotaping.

> Many experienced publishers and copyright attorneys consider the problem of locating copyright owners to be a stimulating challenge. . . . The stimulating challenge of copyright becomes a hopeless maze to the uninitiated. They have neither the experience nor

access, much less personal contact, so necessary in locating and communicating with copyright owners. (Krasilovsky, 1969, p. 417)

That tracking down all the necessary copyright clearances can be a study in frustration was attested to by Gross (1975), who described the runarounds, no answers, no standard policies or prices, and other difficulties encountered during one such attempt.

The prohibitive price of prepared videotapes also posed a problem (for example, Herring, 1980; Hitchens, *Hearings*, 1979). Adams remarked on the fact that schools were charged $750 to $2,000 for a feature-length motion picture in 16mm or three-quarter-inch u-matic videocassette format while retail outlets sold half-inch VHS and Beta video cassettes for $49 to $79 per feature. Similarly, Dana McKenzie Lee (1981), assistant director of the University of Southern California's Humanities Audio Visual Center (HAViC), observed that educational catalogs quote a higher price for videotapes than do video clearinghouses. For example, if $1,000 is budgeted annually per foreign language, only two or three tapes can be purchased per language from educational catalogs during the year. On the other hand, the average price of a foreign-language film through, for example, Video Club of America, is $50. Thus HAViC could buy 20 tapes per language through the clearinghouse.

Troost (1981) illustrated the problem of buying three popular educational TV series in three-quarter-inch videotape format: to purchase 15 of the numerous "Nova" programs would cost $1,500; 13 "Cosmos" shows, $4,160; and, 10 of "Connections," $1,750. That year, an educational institution would have to spend a grand total of $7,310 for just these three series, with little or no budget remaining to purchase other equally important programs.

Another aspect of the economic issue questioned by educators was the validity of copyrights on TV programs paid for with government funds (Essman, 1980; Wylie, 1978). For example, the "Nova" series mentioned above was developed with federal monies, but no automatic off-air taping rights were granted. Rather, a $162.50 per program taping fee was charged, and some shows were sold through Time-Life, Inc. "The Adams Chronicles," with its $6.5 million in federal funding, also had no automatic off-air videotaping rights. The rights to this series were sold to a commercial vendor, Films, Inc. (Adams cited in *Hearings*, 1979).

According to the California Media and Library Educators Association (CMLEA),

many programs of educational value are already financed either through direct grants of public monies or through federal tax credits granted to businesses for program sponsorship. Since compensation from federal funds has been made to these producers, CMLEA endorses the concept that these programs fall within the public domain, and as such may be reproduced under the provisions of section 105 of the copyright law. (*Hearings*, 1979, p. 166; see also Heinemann & Troost, 1979)

Not only are the programs themselves funded, but PBS and similar stations, which both broadcast and produce shows, are largely funded by federal, state, and local governments. In other words, the taxpayer seems to be paying at least twice for such programs. The first payment is through taxes that generate the money to help fund the production. The second payment is through taxes that support the educational institutions that pay for the right to use such programs.

Educators also pointed to the first of the Section 107 fair use criteria: "the purpose and character of the use, including whether such use . . . is for nonprofit educational purposes." The nonprofit, noncommercial intent of schools, it was argued, brought them within the ambit of this fair use factor (see, for example, Adams, *Hearings*, 1979). Steinhilber (*Hearings*, 1979) stated:

We hear comments about piracy, that we are stealing someone's property, et cetera. The education community, when it uses the term fair use and off-the-air taping, is not engaged in profit making endeavors nor is it going to use the materials in question before an audience of the general public. (p. 65)

As for the amount copied, Jerome Miller (*Hearings*, 1979) explained that, given the widely accepted photocopying guidelines, this criterion may not refer to the copying of only a small segment. For example, a short story, short poem, or article may be copied in its entirety. Thus, this issue of taping an entire show may not really be a problem here. Singer (cited in B. Timberg, 1980), a lawyer, saw no difficulty with the partial reproduction of TV programs for constructing an instructional unit; for example, a unit on TV, police, and the law might include segments from "Kojak," "Baretta," and "Starsky and Hutch." Aleinikoff (1980) also considered brief portions of TV programs used for exemplary, analytic, or critical purposes in instructional programs to be fair use, much like a passage from a book (but, see the off-air guidelines discussed in Chapter 4).

Adams (*Hearings*, 1979), on the other hand, acknowledged the difficulty of dealing with this particular criterion. While shows are usually taped in their entirety, even to use a segment requires taping the whole and then editing out the required segment and erasing the rest.

In terms of the fourth factor, economic harm, Kenneth Warren (*Hearings*, 1979), University of Wisconsin TV production coordinator, commented: "I know of no valid information establishing direct correlation between allowing limited nonprofit classroom use, and automatic loss of sale" (p. 82). Adams (*Hearings*, 1979) remarked: "It would be difficult to prove whether videotaping a segment of 'Mork and Mindy' hurts the income of ABC or the affiliate station" (p. 152). He also underlined the fact that "the issue is off-air taping of broadcast television and not the unlawful reproduction of audiovisual materials, available only through commercial vendors. Broadcast television is available free to the entire population" (p. 149).

Free access will not necessarily dry up the incentive to produce, nor will it hurt profits. For example, the assumption is that photocopy users will purchase the original if they have no access to copying. What this ignores is the fact that they may simply forgo using the original ("Photocopying and Fair Use," 1977; see also Breyer, 1970; *Williams & Wilkins*, 1975). In terms of TV, no use of the telecast would seem inconsistent with the desire for a large audience and, therefore, high ratings. Judge Ferguson (*Sony*, 1979) noted in his summary:

> The new technology of videotape recording does bring uncertainty and change which, quite naturally, induce fear. History, however, shows that this fear may be misplaced. As Lewis Wasserman, Chairman of MCA, observed at trial: "[P]eople that have constantly forecast the doom of a particular industry in the entertainment industry have historically been wrong. . . . They forecast the doom of radio stations when television developed on the horizon. Radio stations are more profitable today than they have ever been." Television production by plaintiffs today is more profitable than it has ever been. (p. 695)

Furthermore, there is no guarantee that additional revenues from VTR users will provide the economic incentive for more films to be made.

SUMMARY

Unlike the print medium with its three clearly delineated interest groups, authors, publishers, and users, the television medium includes not only authors, distributors, and users but producers, musicians, directors, and actors, to enumerate but a few. This multiplicity of concerned parties hindered negotiations for the educational off-air taping guidelines finally announced in October 1981 (see Chapter 4 for a discussion of the guidelines). The multitude of parties also, at times, obfuscated the key concerns of the two major factions, that is, copyright proprietors and educators.

Of chief importance to copyright proprietors is whether off-air videotaping decreases profits, both actual and potential. Copyright proprietors express concern that they are being coerced into a situation where they are expected to give but receive nothing in return. They fear that inexpensive reprography will reduce profits to such an extent that funding for new programs will disappear. In addition, inexpensive reprography is seen as a potential danger to existing markets. For example, instead of purchasing several copies of a program from the original source, an educational institution could videorecord the original telecast and reproduce as many copies as it chooses. This type of behavior, if allowed, could lead to the total obliteration of the educational market. Furthermore, they argue, should this occur, producers would be discouraged from producing new educational works. This lack of new educational materials would not be in the public interest.

Off-air taping may also decrease the profits generated by the syndication of old shows on local stations. If people have videotaped the show off the air, the audience for the repeat showing and, therefore, the revenues generated by the rerun are diminished. A related aspect is the threat posed by off-air taping to the prerecorded videotape and videodisc markets. The VTR has a versatility that the videodisc lacks. Furthermore, if the show has been taped off the air free of charge, there is little chance the consumer will pay $50 or more for a prerecorded tape.

Educators deny the allegation that they want "something for nothing." Off-air videotaping is used not to avoid payment but to fill an immediate need. They point to the time lag of six to nine months between the telecast and the availability of its prerecorded videotape for either purchase or lease. Compounding this problem is the lack of indication at the time of telecast as to whether the broadcast will be made available in prepackaged format or purchase or lease at some future date. This time lag and uncertainty result in the loss of optimum teaching moments, for the momentum or timeliness of a show may have dissipated during the six-month lag or be totally lost due to lack of availability.

Furthermore, they argue, students are currently extremely limited in terms of access to televised copyrighted materials and therefore need special access to these works in order to ensure individualized, high quality educational experiences. The broadcast industry itself has contributed to this limited access with its counterprogramming strategies and one-time-only showings. Additional limitations to student access include a program aired during the wrong semester, a student working at the time of broadcast, and the inability of the student to receive the channel at home.

Educators also note the prohibitive price of prerecorded videotapes for the educational market as compared with those on the retail market. Retail outlets and videotape clearinghouses charge $49 to $79 per feature, while educationally oriented distributors charge $250 and up per feature.

Educators also question the need to pay for the use of government-funded programs, such as the "Nova" series. Government funding is defined as either direct grants of public monies for production or federal tax credits granted to businesses sponsoring such programs. In other words, the taxpayer is in essence forced to pay twice. In addition, the question arises whether such programs are in the public domain. The district court's decision in *Schnapper* v. *Foley* (1979), however, seemed to indicate that the use of federal funds by a private firm to produce a film did not automatically preclude that firm from copyrighting the material so produced. Thus, the public domain issue appears to lack strong support.

Both sides acknowledge the importance of the educational use of television. They differ, though, in their assessment of economic harm and their definitions of fair use and public access. The next chapter discusses the issue of public access versus economic considerations apropos of copyright and also analyzes the fair use doctrine and its case law.

3

FAIR USE AND PUBLIC ACCESS

For a better understanding of the problems of educational off-air videotaping, several issues need clarification. One centers around the dual purpose of copyright: public access and economic incentive to creators. Is there a conflict of purpose inherent in the law? Another is the doctrine of fair use itself. What is it? Where did it come from? A third is the courts' view of fair use. How have they interpreted it? When have they allowed its application?

PUBLIC ACCESS VERSUS ECONOMIC INCENTIVE

In *Twentieth Century Music Corporation* v. *Aiken* (1975), the Supreme Court noted that the Copyright Act must be construed in light of its basic purpose when its literal terms have been rendered ambiguous by technological change. What is this basic purpose? According to the constitutional clause empowering Congress to legislate copyright and patent laws, the purpose of those laws is "to promote the progress of science and useful arts [for the public welfare], by securing for limited times to authors and inventors the exclusive right to their respective writings and discoveries [as an economic incentive to create]" (Article I, Section 8, Clause 8).

As the Supreme Court explained in *Mazer* v. *Stein* (1954): "The economic philosophy behind the clause empowering Congress to grant patents and copyrights is the conviction that encouragement of individual effort by personal gain is the best way to advance public welfare through the talents of authors and inventors"

(p. 333). The Supreme Court, discussing the constitutional clause in *Goldstein* v. *State of California* (1973), also said:

> The clause . . . describes both the objective which Congress may seek and the means to achieve it. The objective is to promote the progress of science and the arts. . . . To accomplish its purpose, Congress may grant to authors the exclusive right to the fruits of their respective works . . . to encourage people to devote themselves to intellectual and artistic creation. (p. 133)

Seltzer (1977, 1978) analyzed the clause and found that it either states or implies that

> the products of the intellect are to be especially encouraged;
>
> the way to do this is to give authors a monetary incentive;
>
> there is something about printed [and audio-visual] materials that prevents our relying on the ordinary workings of the marketplace to ensure their production and distribution at appropriate levels;
>
> the economic incentive for the author shall consist in a grant of the exclusive right to make copies of his work;
>
> such controls smack of monopoly;
>
> monopoly is inherently against the public interest because it either denies free access to the work or adds to its cost, or both;
>
> on this account it is to be limited in time; and
>
> this limitation is sufficient to avoid imposing excessive costs, either of price or of access, on the public. (1977, p. 221; 1978, p. 8)

Clapp (1968) called the following excerpt from the House report accompanying the bill for the 1909 Act (which was adopted verbatim by the Senate committee and therefore had the combined authority of both houses) "the classic expression of the relationship" (p. 9) between the public access and economic-incentive-to-create phrases in the constitutional clause:

> The enactment of copyright legislation by Congress under the terms of the Constitution is not based on any natural right that the author has in his writings, for the Supreme Court has held that such rights as he has are purely statutory rights, but upon the ground that the welfare of the public will be served and progress of

science and useful arts will be promoted by securing to authors for limited periods the exclusive right to their writings. The Constitution does not establish copyright, but provides that Congress shall have the power to grant such rights if it thinks best. *Not primarily for the benefit of the author, but primarily for the benefit of the public, such rights are given.* Not that any particular class of citizens, however worthy, may benefit, but because the policy is believed to be for the benefit of the great body of the people, in that it will stimulate writing and invention, to give some bonus to authors and inventors.

In enacting a copyright law, Congress must consider two questions: First, how much will the legislation stimulate the producer and so benefit the public; and second, how much will the monopoly granted be detrimental to the public? The granting of such exclusive rights, under the proper terms and conditions, confers a benefit upon the public that outweighs the evils of the temporary monopoly. (H.R. 2222, pp. 6–7; emphasis added)

This primacy of public access holds true under the 1976 Act as well. In one of its guides to the newest Act, the Copyright Office (1977–1978) stated that the primary purpose of copyright legislation is to nurture the creation and dissemination of intellectual works for the public welfare; its secondary purpose, to reward creators for their contribution to society.

The priority of public access over the creator's reward has also been maintained by the courts. One of the most frequently quoted court reiterations of this priority is from *Fox Film Corporation* v. *Doyal* (1932): "The sole interest of the United States and the primary object in conferring the monopoly lie in the general benefits derived by the public from the labors of authors" (p. 244). In *United States* v. *Paramount Pictures* (1948), the Supreme Court stated: "The copyright law, like the patent statutes, makes reward to the owner a secondary consideration" (p. 253). The Supreme Court reasserted this order of priorities in *Twentieth Century Music* v. *Aiken* (1975): "The immediate effect of our copyright law is to secure a fair return for an 'author's' creative labor. But the ultimate aim is, by this incentive, to stimulate artistic creativity for the general public good" (p. 67). Similar sentiments were expressed in cases such as *Berlin* v. *E. C. Publications, Inc.* (1964), *Meeropol* v. *Nizer* (1978), and *Triangle Publications* v. *Knight-Ridder Newspapers* (1978). On the other hand, Grossman (1977) has argued that just because an author's work benefits society, society does not necessarily have to be considered the primary beneficiary of that work.

Thus, the central elements of the constitutional clause may be stated as follows:

1. The *purpose* of copyright is to benefit society.
2. The *mechanism* by which this purpose is achieved is to be economic.
3. Society's *instrument* in achieving this purpose is to be the author. (Seltzer, 1977, p. 221; 1978, p. 8)

However, achieving the correct balance between the purpose, that is, public access to the freest possible dissemination of knowledge, and the mechanism, economic rewards to creators, has plagued both Congress and the courts.

The Intrinsic Problem

The basic tension underlying copyright law – public access versus economic incentive – stems from the constitutional mandate to Congress. Unfortunately, as Nimmer (1981) has pointed out, due to the secrecy of the committee proceedings at the Constitutional Convention, there is no body of legislative history to help in determining the meaning of this enumerated congressional power. In addition, since the courts have only rarely construed the copyright clause of the Constitution, there is no substantial body of case law presenting a judicial gloss comparable to that found for other constitutional provisions.

Even Madison's (1788/1961) defense of the clause in *The Federalist* offers no useful insight as no conflict between access and economics was foreseen:

> The utility of this power will scarcely be questioned. The copyright of authors has been solemnly adjudged in Great Britain to be a right of common law. The right to useful inventions seems with equal reason to belong to inventors. *The public good fully coincides in both cases with the claims of individuals.* (pp. 271–272; emphasis added)

Probably the most famous elucidation of the public-access-versus-economic-incentive problem is that made by Lord Mansfield in *Sayre* v. *Moore* (1785):

> In deciding . . . we must take care to guard against two extremes equally prejudicial; the one, that men of ability, who have employed their time for the service of the community, may not be deprived of

their just merits, and the reward of their ingenuity and labor; the other, that the world may not be deprived of improvements, nor the progress of the arts be retarded. (p. 139n)

Judge Ferguson (*Sony*, 1979) summed up the public access problem for those with technological interests: "Protection of the public interest requires balancing the need for wide availability of audiovisual works against the need for monetary reward to authors to assure productions of these works" (p. 665). In other words, a way must be found to balance effective and appropriate motivation, reward, and protection for the creation of intellectual works and those technological advances essential to the rapid dissemination and transfer of information so crucial to progress in scientific, technological, and similar endeavors.

Thus, the question becomes: How is public access to be reconciled with a creator's desire – an understandable one – for monetary rewards?

"For Limited Times"

Looking at the constitutional clause phrase by phrase, Nimmer (1981), Seltzer (1977, 1978) and *Classic Film Museum, Inc.* v. *Warner Bros., Inc.* (1979), among others, have suggested that the phrase "for limited times" was included to balance public access and economic reward. The author would have an exclusive monopoly for the time legislated and then the work would pass into the public domain.

The current law, however, grants copyright for a term of the author's life plus 50 years (Section 302). This means at least 50 years would pass before a work would enter into the public domain, assuming the work was copyrighted at the time of the author's death. In the case of a 30-year-old author, it may take well over 85 years before a work would pass into the public domain, considering the growing number of people who live past 65. As public welfare is the chief purpose of copyright legislation, it seems doubtful that a 50- or 85-year wait for access is in the public interest, especially in view of the information explosion and information's rapid growth into "big business."

Patent law, on the other hand, seems more consistent with the constitutional mandate, its term being for an unrenewable 17 years and its exclusivity preventing anyone, even someone who independently creates the identical item, from reaping any rewards from the invention during the patent term. This exclusivity is one of the fundamental distinctions between patents and copyrights. Although Section 106 of the 1976 Act grants the copyright owner exclusive rights to reproduce, prepare derivative works from, distribute copies of, perform, and display the copyrighted work, the exclusivity is limited by Sections 107–118, which include fair use and library reproduction. These limitations, according to the court in *Kepner-Tregoe, Inc.* v. *Carabio* (1979), reflect the paramount importance of the public interest in the advancement of the arts and sciences, an importance that sometimes gives public interest priority over the copyright owner's interest in maximum profit from a creation.

In addition to the differences in duration and nature of the rights granted, patents and copyright also evolved differently regarding standards and procedures for obtaining their respective protection, prevailing judicial interpretations of their respective exclusive domains, and subject matter protected.

Idea–Expression Dichotomy

In *Kepner-Tregoe* (1979), the court suggested that determining exactly what copyright protects should be the first issue addressed. According to the 1976 Act,

> Copyright protection subsists . . . in original works of authorship fixed in any tangible medium of expression, now known or later developed, from which they can be . . . communicated, either directly or with the aid of a machine or device. . . . In no case does copyright protection for an original work of authorship extend to any idea, procedure, process, system, method of operation, concept, principle, or discovery, regardless of the form in which it is described, explained, illustrated, or embodied in such work. (Section 102)

In other words, "unlike a patent, a copyright gives no exclusive right to the art disclosed; protection is given only to the expression of the idea—not the idea itself" (*Mazer* v. *Stein*, 1954, p. 333). As the court explained in *Wainwright Securities Inc.* v. *Wall Street Transcript Corporation* (1977): "What is protected is the manner of expression, the author's analysis or interpretation of events, the way he structures his material and marshals facts, his choice of words, and the emphasis he gives to particular developments" (p. 404).

Baker v. *Selden* (1879) serves as one of the early precedents for establishing this dichotomy in copyright protection. In 1859, Selden copyrighted *Selden's Condensed Ledger, or Bookkeeping*

Simplified, which explained the particular system and included blank forms. When Baker began selling similar forms for the same system, Selden filed against Baker for alleged copyright infringement, but Baker denied the charges on the grounds that the matter allegedly infringed was not "a lawful subject of copyright" (p. 100). The original decree was for Selden, the plaintiff, but Baker appealed. The Supreme Court reversed the circuit court's decision and dismissed the original complainant's bill, holding that "blank accountbooks are not the subject of copyright" (p. 107). In reaching this decision, the Court commented, "Where the truths of a science or the methods of an art are the common property of the whole world, any author has the right to express the one, or explain and use the other, in his own way" (pp. 100-101). In other words, everyone has the right to use an idea as long as its expression is not plagiarized.

Judge Manton, in *Shipman* v. *R.K.O. Radio Pictures, Inc.* (1938), noted, "Ideas are not copyrightable but the sequence of events is" (p. 214). Again, in *Bradbury* v. *Columbia Broadcasting System* (1961), the court reaffirmed that "the means of expressing an idea is subject to copyright protection" (p. 382). Also, in *Kepner-Tregoe* (1979) the court maintained that "it is the strong policy of copyright not to protect ideas. Free interchange of thought is paramount" (p. 131). Later in this decision, the court expanded upon its statement: "There is nothing in the law that precludes one author from saving time and effort through the labors of others. This waste of energy the ban on copyright of ideas prevents" (p. 134, but see *Toksvig* v. *Bruce Publishing Company,* 1950).

The idea–expression dichotomy is thought a solution to the access–economics dilemma because "ideas which may be of public interest are not subject to copyright" (*Sid & Marty Krofft Television Productions* v. *McDonald's Corporation,* 1977, p. 108). In other words,

> it is an axiom of copyright law that the protection granted to a copyrighted work extends only to the particular expression of the idea and never to the idea itself.... This principle attempts to reconcile two competing social interests: rewarding an individual's creativity and effort while at the same time permitting the nation to enjoy the benefits and progress from use of the same subject matter. (*Krofft,* p. 101)

Similarly, in *Franklin Mint Corporation* v. *National Wildlife Art Exchange* (1978), the court explained, "To reconcile the competing societal interests inherent in copyright law, copyright protection has been extended only to the particular *expression* of an idea and not to the idea itself" (p. 723). Further support for this stance came from those who defined fair use in terms of the dichotomy. For example, in *Sheldon* v. *Metro-Goldwyn Pictures Corporation* (1936), the court stated, "It is convenient to define such a use [referring to fair use] by saying that others may 'copy' the 'theme,' or 'ideas,' or the like, of a work, but not its 'expression' " (p. 335). In other words, it is in the public interest to have *ideas* freed from any type of exclusive usage arrangement, whereas a monopoly on the *expression* of those ideas is in the creator's interest. However, as the lower court noted in *Nichols* v. *Universal Pictures Corporation* (1929), while ideas are not in and of themselves protected, at times it is difficult to distinguish between idea and expression. Where does the idea end and the expression begin? This line is especially blurred when dealing with visual media.

> In general, the democratic dialogue – a self-governing people's participation in the marketplace of ideas – is adequately served if the public has access to an author's ideas, and such loss to the dialogue as results from inaccessibility to an author's "expression" is counterbalanced by the greater public interest in the copyright system. But this conclusion requires reappraisal if there are certain areas of creativity where the "idea" of a work contributes almost nothing to the democratic dialogue, and it is only its expression which is meaningful . . . as anyone who attempts to describe the "idea" of the *Mona Lisa* or of Michelangelo's *Moses* must realize. (Nimmer, 1970, p. 1197; see also Lawrence, 1980b; Nimmer, 1981)

So how does one separate the idea from the picture expressing it? Perhaps an answer to this question would also help solve the question of off-air videotaping.

Constitutional Amendments

According to this approach, the fair use doctrine is not the user's only means of reasonable access to materials. Its supporters favor the direct application of the First and Ninth Amendments. The First Amendment states that "Congress shall make no law . . . abridging the freedom of speech, or of the press." The Ninth Amendment – "the enumeration in the Constitution of certain rights, shall not be construed to deny or disparage others retained by the people" – is interpreted as including the right of access to information. An underlying tenet of the constitutional argument is that the right of access to information and the rights of political participation, free speech, and so forth are interrelated. Consider, how can a citizen effectively exercise the latter rights without a knowledge of the facts pertaining to a particular topic? How often have you gone into the voting booth wishing you had better access to information about the issues? However, the disputatious dialogue generated by this approach to strengthening the public access argument for fair use of copyrighted works has further complicated an already tangled web.

Opponents of this approach point out that claiming free access for the public welfare under the ambit of the First Amendment changes access from an underlying constitutional goal into a distinct criterion. Furthermore, this approach muddles the place of copyright and the First Amendment in our system. Finally, the First Amendment and its underlying purpose of free speech do not justify carte blanche expropriation of copyrighted materials, even for "good causes" such as education. As one court commented: "The first amendment is not a license to trammel on legally recognized rights in intellectual property" (*Dallas Cowboys Cheerleaders* v. *Scoreboard Posters*, 1979, p. 323).

Despite increasing attempts to invoke a First Amendment defense in copyright infringement cases, the courts have been wary of accepting it lest First Amendment arguments come to supersede the protective role of copyright (see, for example, *Italian Book Corporation* v. *American Broadcasting Companies*, 1978; *Wainwright*, 1978; but compare *Red Lion Broadcasting Co., Inc.* v. *FCC*, 1969; *Rosemont Enterprises, Inc.* v. *Random House, Inc.*, 1967; *Time Incorporated* v. *Bernard Geis Associates*, 1968; *Triangle* v. *Knight-Ridder*, 1978). The courts' reluctance to accept First Amendment arguments has underlined the constitutional puzzle presented by the copyright clause and the First Amendment. Copyright protection results in a partial monopoly over expression, which may be considered an unconstitutional abridgement of First Amendment rights. If so, then copyright must be held as unconstitutional since the First Amendment supersedes any prior inconsistent law.

In *Wainright* (1977), the court declared: "Conflicts between interests protected by the first amendment and the copyright laws thus far have been resolved by application of the fair use doctrine" (p. 403). But the court went on to reach its decision through the idea–expression dichotomy approach.

Both the courts and legal commentators have seemed to agree that the idea–expression dichotomy provides the best solution to the copyright clause–First Amendment dilemma. In cases such as

Krofft v. *McDonald's* (1977) and *Schnapper* v. *Foley* (1979), for example, the courts turned to the idea–expression dichotomy as a means of resolving competition between copyright and the First Amendment. They both indicated that since copyright is limited to protecting expression, it does not endanger the "marketplace of ideas" guaranteed by the First Amendment. Nimmer (1981) thought that if copyright protected ideas "there would be a serious encroachment upon First Amendment values" (section 1.10). According to Brittin (1978), copyright does not limit the First Amendment because "copyrighting a work does not preclude others from using it or dealing with the same subject matter; rather it precludes reproduction of a similar text" (p. 86). Jacqueline Shapiro (1980) differentiated between First Amendment rights and copyright law on the basis of mass versus individual communication, that is, the creation and dissemination of expression: The First Amendment protects speech and press, copyright protects tangible individual communications.

The court noted in *Triangle* (1978) that both copyright and the First Amendment "are oriented toward the preservation of an atmosphere conducive to the interchange of ideas" (pp. 35–36). However, the court went on to warn that when copyright and the First Amendment do operate at cross-purposes, the First Amendment supersedes the scope of copyright law. But as the *Rosemont* (1966) court cautioned, the First Amendment does apply to copyright when copyright protection is used to interfere with the public's right to information of general interest, that is, when copyright is used as a tool of censorship. Similarly, applying Alexander Meiklejohn's "public speech theory," which has as its central concept free accessibility to all information of public interest and concern, Oakes (1978) declared that any attempt by an author or composer to suppress speech through the use of his copyright or property right is a violation of the First Amendment.

Thus, copyright laws and the First Amendment may be reconciled by saying that the First Amendment prevents copyright from returning to its early function as censor. However, Lyman Patterson (1975) argued that permitting copyright in its present form to exist for TV broadcasts creates an historical first: censorship power given to licensees of the federal government. He opined that the threat to First Amendment rights posed by copyright for TV broadcasts is obscured by the notion that copyright is an author's right. Returning to copyright's English origins (see the historical discussion in Chapter 1), Patterson claimed that the idea of an author's right is a legal fiction.

Questioning Copyright's Concept

Haunting the discussion of copyright is the key question of whether the public's interest in maximum information dissemination is best served by protecting intellectual property rather than permitting free access to copyrighted materials. In other words, is copyright indeed a legitimate instrument of public policy (see Seltzer, 1977)?

According to Henry (1975), the answer is no. Copyright as a public policy for information creation and dissemination is no longer suitable for technological societies such as ours. However, Henry built his anticopyright case on the assumption that the basic belief of copyright was that ideas are property to be managed according to proprietary concepts. As the discussion above of the idea–expression dichotomy showed, ideas are not copyrightable. Thus Henry's arguments lack strong support.

Rosenfield (1975) argued that copyright is becoming antiquated and irrelevant for vast areas of intellectual creativity, productivity, and use. He therefore supported fair use as a constitutional right guaranteeing public access to copyrighted information.

Toffler (1980), although he did not discuss copyright per se, has lent some support to the querying of its continued legitimacy as an instrument of public policy. He maintained that modern industrial society developed a host of organizations that had to work within a framework of predictable rules; hence the need for laws to bring the information, social, and technical spheres into harmony. This description seems apropos in light of copyright's historical background, for the law has been an attempt to harmonize the technology of printing and the increase of information with the demands of society. Past attitudes, as Toffler has pointed out, are no longer appropriate; it is time to develop new ideas and concepts better suited to the modern world of technology and communication.

Copyright has been profoundly affected by its inability to accommodate new technologies such as off-air videotaping, and its usefulness in a "third wave" (postindustrial) society is in question. Ringer (1977b) referred to copyright's difficulty in resolving issues of a postindustrial nature. And Judge Ferguson's *Sony* (1979) decision has been described as an indication that the old copyright system of control is breaking down in the face of the current technological revolution (Roberts, 1980). More narrowly, the UCLA "Project" (1968) concluded: "the doctrine of fair use, at least as presently construed, ought not survive the reprographic revolution" (p. 954).

In answering his own question on copyright's legitimacy, Seltzer (1977) identified two approaches. The first is based on the traditional notions of private property argued and decided upon in cases such as *Millar* (1769), *Donaldson* (1774), and *Wheaton* (1834). Copyright is seen as either protecting the author's existing "natural rights" or as establishing rights where none existed before. The second approach relates to the original question of whether an economic incentive is in society's best interests. This approach views copyright as "an unwarranted monopoly" originating from, for example, "religious censorship, royal printing patents, state control of political dissent, and the protection of special interests like those of artisans in certain guilds or those of booksellers in cartel-like associations" (p. 217) and therefore inherently suspect. Three arguments are used in this approach to defend the stand that economic incentive may not be the most efficient method for promoting the progress of science and the arts.

In the first argument, copyright is equated with a monopoly resulting in high prices not offset by any public advantage, in which case copyright allows for excessive profits to the owner (Breyer, 1970). In the second argument, the publisher, in the role of intermediary between author and public, is seen as altering the economic facts, especially those of author incentive. This argument also receives support from Lyman Patterson (1972), who attributed the unsatisfactory copyright situation to the fact that legislators have no sound theory of copyright law. According to Patterson, legislators lack a copyright theory because they persist in treating copyright as a protection for the author rather than as a protection for the publisher. Yet protecting publishers is copyright's major function. Its essence is the right of exclusive publication; copyright prevents another publisher from publishing that same work. And while the author receives royalties from the publisher, the exclusivity of publication does not really matter to the author. Regardless of how many publishers pay the royalty fee for a particular work, the author is paid. The exclusivity of publication is only more profitable for the publisher. This focus on authors' rather than publishers' rights is an historical fluke rather than a product of logical thinking. The third argument charges that new technology has changed the format and boundaries of public access, making copyright obsolete (see Henry, 1975; Toffler, 1980).

Taken together, the arguments suggest that copyright is a monopoly not in the best interests of the public. If it were removed, then, à la Adam Smith, the market would produce goods at the lowest cost possible (Seltzer, 1977). Breyer (1970) has offered the additional argument that postulations of rewarding creators for lasting works of social value and contributions to the general progress are weakened by the fact that the rewards usually go to popular works. Many serious works of great social value have small audiences and therefore small economic rewards.

Seltzer (1977) has refuted these arguments to show copyright's validity. First, he found no examples of economic benefits from a noncopyright system. Second, a number of the conventional microeconomic rules do not appear to apply. For example, what appears to be a monopoly is actually competition: a new novel competes against both old and new ones. Also, prices are not kept high; paperback versions are usually available shortly after the hardcover novels are published. Third, educators do not question the validity of copyright but argue that education's superior claim for free access could be honored without hurting the copyright owners. Finally, Congress has not abandoned the scheme: "Decisions undermining authors' copyrights in favor of other social goals discouraged the creativity necessary for cultural development"; therefore "Congress has consistently viewed the promotion of individual creativity as the best means of ensuring the benefits of continued technological change to the public" (Shapiro, 1980, pp. 1043; 1046).

Breyer (1970) has noted an additional argument in favor of economic incentive: the author's "moral rights." In other words, "it is certainly not agreeable to natural justice, that a stranger should reap the beneficial pecuniary produce of another man's work" (*Millar*, 1769, p. 218). But, Breyer questioned the need to reward a creator beyond the "persuasion price," the price at which the creator agrees to produce his work. This sentiment is echoed by the CONTU (1979) final report, which suggested that a copyright should not grant anyone more economic power than is necessary to achieve the incentive to work. Despite his misgivings, Breyer concluded that copyright should not be abolished but warned against its unnecessary extension.

THE DOCTRINE OF FAIR USE

The doctrine of fair use actually originated with the judiciary. Given copyright's constitutional mandate of promoting progress in the arts and sciences the courts soon realized that a strict construction of the copyright owner's exclusive rights would, in many instances, inhibit the dissemination of knowledge, thus defeating copyright's raison d'être. Therefore, the courts slowly evolved a concept of "fair use," the use in certain instances of copyrighted materials without the copyright owner's explicit permission.

Fair use as a concept was introduced by Lord Ellenborough in *Cary* v. *Kearsley* (1802):

> That part of the work of one author is found in another, is not of itself piracy, or sufficient to support an action; a man may fairly adopt part of the work of another: he may so make use of another's labours for the promotion of science, and the benefit of the public: but having done so, the question will be, Was the matter so taken *used fairly* with that view. (p. 680, emphasis added)

Lord Eldon (*Wilkins* v. *Aiken*, 1810) stated: "There is no doubt, that a man cannot under the pretence of quotation, publish either the whole or part of another's work; though he may use, what it is in all cases very difficult to define, *fair quotation*" (p. 164, emphasis added). In the same decision, he also spoke of "legitimate use" (p. 164). Justice Story, in *Folsom* v. *Marsh* (1841), mentioned "justifiable use" and "fair and reasonable criticism" (p. 344). The first reported use of fair use per se is in the English case *Lewis* v. *Fullarton* (1839); however, it was first recognized as a legal doctrine in the Massachusetts case *Lawrence* v. *Dana* (1869): "The defense of 'a fair use' is not tenable in this case" (p. 44). It remained a judicial limitation on copyright exclusivity until its incorporation into the present Copyright Act as Section 107.

Needham (1959) has offered another approach to the origins of fair use, noting that three sources for the doctrine are usually cited. The first source is based on the presumption that the author's intention was to allow certain uses of his work. McDonald (1962) and Wylie (1978) seem to have adopted this viewpoint in their "golden rule" approach to defining fair use: Take from others only to the extent and in a manner that you would not mind, if they so took from you, were you the copyright owner. A similar approach is suggested by Latman (1958/1963): "Would the reasonable copyright owner have consented to the use?" (p. 15). Unfortunately, these simplistic theorems are usually not supported by court decisions involving fair use (see discussion following). Needham called this source a "legal fiction" that could cause misunderstandings, an opinion supported by Nimmer (1981): "It is sometimes suggested that fair use is predicated on the implied or tacit consent of the author. This is manifestly a fiction" (section 13.05).

The second source is based on the legal principle *de minimus non curat lex* – the law does not concern itself with trifles. Commissioner Davis, in *Williams & Wilkins* (1972), mentioned that some courts hold that fair use is but an application of the *de minimus* principle. In *Meredith Corporation* v. *Harper & Row, Publishers* (1974), Judge Owen noted that fair use was originally based on the assumption that an individual, while freely using unprotected materials, might be allowed to copy an insignificant portion of copyrighted material. The doctrine then developed to permit more than insignificant copying of copyrighted material when such copying was clearly seen as in the public interest and serving the underlying tenet of the constitutional mandate. *De minimus* and fair use was also commented upon in *Mathews Conveyer Company* v. *Palmer-Bee Company* (1943) and *Mills Music, Inc.* v. *State of Arizona* (1979), among others. But as Needham pointed out, this does not adequately explain fair use involving a large quantity of copying. A similar point was noted in *Rosemont* v. *Random House* (1966), in which the court explained that extensive verbatim copying or paraphrasing of copyrighted material does not satisfy the concept of reasonableness that is at the heart of fair use.

The *Rosemont* (1966) court did, however, support the third source, constitutional policy: "The fundamental justification for the privilege lies in the constitutional purpose in granting copyright protection in the first instance" (p. 719). According to Latman (*Hearings*, 1979), this source has become the popular theoretical basis for the doctrine. A constitutional source is also championed by Rosenfield (1975), who stressed that the constitutional dimension of fair use must be protected by both Congress and the judiciary. He maintained that fair use was directly protected by the Constitution and had further protection under the penumbra of the First and Ninth Amendments. This protection covers "the right of reasonable access to our cultural, educational, scientific, historical, technical, and intellectual heritage" (p. 791). Nevertheless, as discussed earlier, the use of a defense based on the constitutional amendments is not readily accepted by the courts in all cases, although the idea–expression dichotomy is often used as the criterion for supporting such a defense.

Defining the Doctrine

Among the solutions proposed for reconciling public access and economic incentive, the doctrine of fair use has received the greatest attention, especially from those involved in the debate over educational uses of copyrighted material. According to Hayes (1978), this interest in fair use stems from its underlying assumption that at some point the balance between access and incentive fails to maximize information dissemination. In other words, fair use presupposes that certain instances require greater access to copyrighted materials but, at the same time, will not discourage creators from producing further copyrighted works. Science, medicine, law, history, and biography are among the fields most often affected by this need for maximum information dissemination.

However, as Saul Cohen (1955) wryly noted: "There is one proposition about fair use on which there is widespread agreement: it is not easy to decide what is and what is not fair use" (p. 52), a sentiment echoed by Commissioner Davis: "What constitutes 'fair use' cannot be defined with precision" (*Williams & Wilkins*, 1972, p. 678; see also *Dallas Cowboys Cheerleaders* v. *Scoreboard Posters*, 1979). Even Ball's (1944) oft-quoted definition—"a privilege in other than the owner of a copyright to use the copyrighted material in a reasonable manner without his consent, notwithstanding the monopoly granted to the owner by the copyright" (p. 244)— proves vague as it does not explain what constitutes a "reasonable manner." This lack of specificity in defining fair use, of course, adds to the general feeling of frustration when dealing with the doctrine.

The statutory recognition of fair use by no means clarifies matters, for Congress failed to define the doctrine in Section 107. In fact, the issue has been thrown back to the courts for decision. However, since the Copyright Act does not specify a definition of the doctrine, the courts will be forced to consult the legislative history. The Supreme Court, in *United States of America* v. *American Trucking Associations* (1940), indicated that when a statute's wording is sufficient in and of itself to determine the legislative purpose, the court should follow the "plain meaning." Yet, the court indicated that when this produces unreasonable results plainly at odds with the legislation, the courts should look at the legislative purpose rather than the literal wording. Thus, "when aid to construction of the meaning of words, as used in the statute, is available, there certainly can be no 'rule of law' which forbids its use, however clear the words may appear on 'superficial examination'" (pp. 543–544).

Cardozo (1976–1977) explained legislative history to include statements by the proponents, witnesses, congressional committees, and legislators on the floor of the legislature. He also noted that today it is extremely rare for a court not to consult the legislative history. Billings (1977), however, referred to Professor Reed Dickerson's authoritative view that legislative history should not be created for the purpose of helping courts interpret and apply statutes. Yet this appears to be what has occurred in copyright. The 1976 Act cannot be readily applied to educational off-air videotaping without the aid of the House and Senate reports, a situation which exists for all classroom applications of fair use. To further snarl an already enmeshed cycle, legislative history does not have the force of law, nor are the courts bound by it.

Moving to the legislative history, H.R. 94-1476 (1976) is the original House report, S. 94-473 (1975) the original Senate report, and H.R. 94-1733 (1976) the conference report that ironed out the few differences between the first two. In actuality, all three were very similar in wording, at times even verbatim.

The reports discussed the definition of fair use; disappointingly, however, they gave no precise definition of the doctrine. As H.R. 94-1476 and S. 94-473 explained, "Since the doctrine is an equitable rule of reason, no generally applicable definition is possible, and each case raising the question must be decided on its own facts" (p. 65; p. 62, respectively). The congressional intent of this vagueness was justified on the basis of technological change:

> The bill endorses the purpose and general scope of the judicial doctrine of fair use, but there is no disposition to freeze the doctrine in the statute, especially during a period of rapid technological change. . . . The courts must be free to adapt the doctrine to particular situations on a case-by-case basis. Section 107 is intended to restate the present judicial use, not to change, narrow, or enlarge it in any way. (H.R. 94-1476, p. 66; similarly, S. 94-473, p. 62)

But despite this general disclaimer of no intent to change existing case law, legal commentators have found changes. For instance, Parris (1977) observed that the specifics discussed in the committee reports may have expanded the current fair use concept, while Freid (1977) noted that the reports provided more guidance than ever before on what constitutes minimum standards of fair use in selected circumstances.

While giving no concrete definition of fair use, the reports did quote from the *Register's 1961 Report* various, but "by no means exhaustive," examples of what the courts might regard as fair use. Included were "reproduction by a teacher or student of a small part of a work to illustrate a lesson" and "quotation of short passages in a scholarly or technical work, for illustration or clarification of the author's observation" (cited in H.R. 94-1476, p. 65; S. 94-473, pp. 61–62). As with these two, the other examples are also instances of fragmentary copying, not copying of a whole work. The Senate's report noted that "classroom copying that exceeds the legitimate teaching aims such as filling in missing information or bringing a subject up to date would go beyond the proper bounds of fair use" (p. 65).

Latman (1958/1963) and Yankwich (1954) outlined basic situations involving fair use:

1. Incidental use of copyrighted material, such as a fortuitous inclusion in a news broadcast (for example, *Italian Book Corp.* v. *ABC*, 1978), or inclusion of a few lines of lyrics in an article (for example, *Karll* v. *Curtis Publishing Co.*, 1941) is considered fair use.
2. Review and criticism seem to be universally agreed upon as fair use for there are apparently no reported U.S. cases involving serious criticism. Indeed, in *Loew's Inc.* v. *Columbia Broadcasting System, Inc.* (1955), the court stated: "Criticism is an important and proper exercise of fair use. . . . Critics may quote extensively for the purpose of illustration and comment" (p. 310).
3. Parody and burlesque seem to be considered fair use in most instances (for example, *Elsmere Music* v. *National Broadcasting Company*, 1980; *Hill* v. *Whalen & Martell, Inc.*, 1914; but compare *Loew's* v. *CBS*, 1955).
4. Scholarly works and compilations is an area that sharply contrasts the right to use and the right to copy, especially in the fields of science, law, medicine, history, and biography, where research is an important foundation (for example, *Rosemont* v. *Random House*, 1966).
5. Personal or private uses find case law silent. Why this is so was not clear.
6. News is the center of some cases. The facts themselves are open to fair use (for example, *Wainwright* v. *Wall Street Transcript*, 1978; *Iowa State University Research Foundation* v. *American Broadcasting Companies*, 1980).
7. Use of direct quotations in litigation does not have any reported cases.
8. Use for nonprofit or governmental purposes is not automatically fair use (for example, *Wihtol* v. *Crow*, 1962).

Nonetheless, the outline still leaves fair use without a precise definition.

Section 107

In the absence of a specific definition of fair use, the criteria listed in Section 107 become the focus of attention, as they seem to provide general guidelines for applying the fair use doctrine. These criteria closely resemble those originally enunciated by Justice Story in *Folsom* (1841):

> In short, we must often, in deciding questions of this sort, look to the nature and objects of the selections made, the quantity and value of the materials used, and the degree in which the use may prejudice the sale, or diminish the profits, or supersede the objects, of the original work. (p. 348)

Similar criteria were noted by the courts in such cases as *Mathews Conveyer Co.* v. *Palmer-Bee Co.* (1943), *Meredith* v. *Harper & Row* (1974), *New York Tribune, Inc.* v. *Otis & Co.* (1941), and *Shapiro, Bernstein & Co., Inc.* v. *P. F. Collier & Son Co.* (1934).

These criteria, though, were meant as examples of the types of factors to be considered for they were introduced by the words "shall include." According to Section 101 of the Act, "Definition": "The terms 'including' and 'such as' are illustrative and not limitative." But these four fair use criteria, despite congressional intent, seem to have become "gospel." For example, Ivan Bender (1980) has stated that they must be met, even though one or more of them may predominate.

How else can the fair use criteria be delineated? The third factor, "portion used," for example, could be considered as five different questions:

> (1) How much was "taken?" (2) how much did it amount to relative to the "work" it was taken from? (3) how much did it amount to in relation to the work which it was incorporated into? (4) how important was it to the "work" it was taken from? (5) how important is it to the work which it was incorporated into? (Johnston, 1980, p. 114)

Saul Cohen (1955) analyzed the case decisions and discovered that the courts considered eight elements, any one of which may be decisive in a particular case:

> (1) the type of use involved; (2) the intent with which it was made; (3) its effect on the original work; (4) the amount of the user's labor involved; (5) the benefit gained by him; (6) the nature of the works involved; (7) the amount of material used; and (8) its relative value. (p. 53)

In a similar analysis, Needham (1959) distilled 16 key questions:

1. Did the user's work comprise a large part of the author's work?
2. Did the user take a large portion of the author's work?
3. Did the user take a valuable portion of the author's work?
4. Did the user save much labor by using the author's work?
5. Did the user add little to the author's work?
6. Was the user's use central instead of incidental?
7. Could the user's work serve as a substitute for the author's work?
8. Did the user circulate his work to the public?
9. Did the user charge for his work, or get advertising benefits?
10. Did the user copy from a nonscientific work?
11. Was the user's work nonscientific?
12. Was the user's work designed for other than students?
13. Is the author's work one which was not designed for copying?
14. Is the author's work original, and not merely a compilation?
15. Did the user intend to infringe?*
16. Did the user fail to acknowledge the source? (pp. 81-1)†

William Hart (1981) identified three factors often influencing the courts but not listed in Section 107: public interest; degree of creativity in the work; and enforceability of the copyright. Thus, the four criteria actually listed in Section 107 should not be considered the sole factors, although they are critical.

Just as Section 107 failed to provide a precise definition of fair use, so did it fail to specify the order of applying the four criteria cited and the weight to be attached to each. Most commentators have indicated that the fourth factor – economic harm – should be considered first (for example, Johnston, 1980; Nimmer, 1981; Seltzer, 1977), a factor also noted in *Sony* (1979) and commented upon in *Williams & Wilkins* (1972). Seltzer (1977) suggested reordering the criteria as follows: 4, 2, 1, 3. This order, he claimed, gives a more logical picture of how copyright actually works. Hayes (1978), however, conducted a small survey to determine the courts' view of weighting factors. He found that the third factor – amount and substantiality – is mentioned most often. Purpose of use and economic effect are next, with nature of the work least important.

*According to Section 504 of the 1976 Act, unintentional infringement may result in a reduction of damages awarded, but it is not an adequate fair use defense in and of itself.

†Acknowledging the source does not, taken alone, necessarily constitute a fair use.

Freid's (1977) analysis of the criteria determined that the first—the nature of the use—and the fourth are the two most often used by the courts as decisive factors because they are closely related to the purpose of copyright laws. The courts will often allow use of copyrighted materials to help the progress of the arts and sciences, despite any infringements upon the copyright proprietor's exclusive rights, because the use furthers the purpose of copyright (for example, *Rosemont,* 1967; *Time* v. *Bernard Geis,* 1968). The remaining two criteria—the nature of the copyrighted work and the amount and substantiality of the portion used—have a secondary effect and become important only when the two major ones are inapplicable or indecisive. In fact, the former is only important in relation to the criterion of economic harm. For if the copyrighted work does not have a "useful" nature, that is, if it does not further artistic or scientific progress or the public interest, then the economic effect factor will lose its significance as a fair use determinant.

Furthermore, Freid discovered a pattern in the interrelationship of the two major criteria (purpose of use and economic effect). In any given situation, the two criteria interact in one of four ways, depending on whether the use is positive (that is, furthers progress in the arts and sciences) as compared to an ordinary one and whether the use will have a detrimental economic effect on the copyright owner and thus undermine copyright's incentive system. The four interactions are

1. detrimental effect–ordinary use
2. no detrimental effect–positive use
3. no detrimental effect–ordinary use
4. detrimental effect–positive use.

The first two types of interaction have offered the courts little difficulty (see, for example, *Henry Holt and Company* v. *Liggett and Myers Tobacco Company,* 1938; *Rosemont,* 1967). In the third category, the courts have looked to other factors, such as amount used. Cases involving parody are typical of this category (see for example, *Berlin* v. *E. C. Publications,* 1964; *Loew's* v. *CBS.* 1958). The last category proves the most difficult for the courts because the effect and use call for divergent results. Since the use is a positive one, it should be allowed; but since its effect is detrimental to the copyright owner, it should be forbidden (see, for example, *Williams & Wilkins,* 1975).

Conversely, Hayes (1978) identified four problems attached to the economic effect factor. First is the problem of proving economic harm, which he claimed, is grounded in circular reasoning: "The market loss attributable to a fair use can only be measured if the unauthorized use is an unfair one; if the copying is a fair use then, by definition, there is no market loss" (p. 107). Second is the assumption that the copyright owner expects a reward; but copyright "only presupposes that *if* money is to be earned from a creation, it belongs to the copyright owner" (p. 109). Third, since the copying effects of all who might be defendants are not aggregated, what may appear *de minimus* might actually be substantial. Fourth, the courts sometimes excuse unauthorized copyright uses because there is little net economic effect apparent. However, the reason that a more substantial economic loss did not appear may be due to an increased burden on the paying customer.

Other criticisms of Section 107 are directed at Congress for not rethinking the fair use doctrine and merely adopting the judicial approach regardless of inherent shortcomings. Also, the introductory language of Section 107 was criticized for possibly changing traditional fair use because of the six illustrative purposes of fair use cited in Section 107: criticism, comment, news reporting, teaching, scholarship, and research. Only the first three are traditionally accepted as fair uses grounded in the First Amendment. The remaining three are broad education-related exemptions not necessarily covered by First Amendment arguments. In fact, teaching was included in the 1976 Act because of extensive educational lobbying spurred by the concern that some copying was necessary for the full exploitation of technology as a teaching aid in the classroom. Prior to this, teaching had not been held as a justification for copying substantial portions of a work for classroom use (see the discussion of *Macmillan Co.* v. *King*, 1914, and *Wihtol* v. *Crow*, 1962, following). In other words, although commentators may have recognized teaching, scholarship, and research as fair use, the courts have not given them blanket approval.

Yet another criticism of Section 107 is that it failed to distinguish between fair use and exempted use. Fair use has been defined as accommodating the relationships within copyright and therefore falling under judicial jurisdiction; exempted use as balancing interests outside the copyright scheme and therefore falling under legislative jurisdiction (Seltzer, 1977). However, in Section 107, instead of addressing itself to defining fair use or explaining the fair use doctrine and its application in light of modern technology, Congress discussed fair use as a means of solving the photocopying issue as it pertains to educational purposes, which is an exempted use. In other words, fair use is discussed in the context of a particular exemption, thus blurring the line between the two uses.

Furthermore, in discussing Section 107, H.R. 94-1476 asserted that a specific "exemption" freeing certain copying of copyrighted materials for educational and scholarly purposes from copyright control is not justified. But in Section 108, "Reproduction by Libraries," the 1976 Act did just that. Congress seems to have used the terms *fair use* and *exempted use* synonymously, thus adding to the confusion.

Besides blurring the distinction between fair and exempted uses, the preoccupation with photocopying may have contributed to the failure to delineate the boundaries of off-air videotaping apropos of fair use. H.R. 94-1476 explained that "the problem of off-the-air taping for nonprofit classroom use of copyrighted audiovisual works incorporated in radio and television broadcasts has proved to be difficult to resolve" (p. 71). It also stated that fair use "has some limited application in this area" (p. 71); that is, under appropriate circumstances, fair use could apply, for example, to showing a short excerpt from a motion picture for criticism or comment. Nevertheless, the issue needed further exploration.

Finally, the report suggested the establishment of guidelines agreed to by the concerned parties, much as had been done for books, periodicals, and music. This type of guideline, however, merely acts as a statement of the minimum educational fair use, not the maximum. Thus, some categories of copying may be permitted, although not stated in the guidelines. In addition, the guidelines are subject to revision. These limitations raise questions about the usefulness of such guidelines. At the time the Act was passed, agreement could not be reached on defining minimum fair use levels for off-air taping.

The Senate's S. 94–473 offered a slightly more specific approach than the House's report, but it too was couched in advisory language. For example, in discussing the nature of the copyrighted work, the Senate pointed out that "consumables" such as workbooks should be considered differently than newspaper articles for fair use purposes, and "in general terms it could be expected that the doctrine of fair use would be applied strictly to the classroom reproduction of entire works, such as . . . audiovisual works including motion pictures" (p. 64).

The one concrete example of fair use educational off-air taping in the legislative history is the Senate committee's discussion of off-air taping by individual schools in remote areas. Using Alaska, with its many time zones and transmission difficulties, as an example, the committee indicated that it believed that the off-air videotaping of an instructional television transmission for the purpose of delayed viewing of the program by students in such a remote area constitutes a fair use. Furthermore, a remote school such as described would only be able to retain the recording for a limited time. However, the committee also cautioned that it did not intend to suggest that off-air taping for convenience was of itself considered fair use.

Probably the only issue Section 107 did resolve is whether or not fair use constitutes an excused infringement. The Act specifically stated that fair use is not considered a copyright infringement.

THE COURTS AND FAIR USE

The failure of Section 107 to define and delineate fair use adequately, especially for educational off-air videotaping, has shifted the focus back to the courts. However, there are few litigated cases dealing with fair use and education, and even fewer concerning fair use, education, and audio-visual materials. Also, the traditional application of fair use criteria is undergoing serious reconsideration due to current technological advances and their impact, both actual and potential.

Despite these misgivings, the fact remains that the "traditional" court interpretations of fair use are still the standard. As Section 107 was a restatement of the current judicial doctrine at the time and not meant to freeze it, the old case law maintains its validity. Thus, both old and new decisions must be consulted in determining what the courts consider fair use.

The discussion below first investigates the courts' interpretations of the four criteria, then focuses special attention on two cases involving individual teachers, and finally analyzes videotape recording–related cases.*

---

*Williams & Wilkins (1975), which centered on library photocopying, is not examined independently of the general discussion because "decisions of equally divided courts are res judicata as between the parties, but they do not bind other courts as to principles of law" ("Photocopying and Fair Use," 1977, p. 854). In addition, Section 108 of the new Act and the guidelines for photocopying books and journals in its legislative history were designed to resolve the problem posed by this case. For a discussion of this case see, for example, Blackwell (1974), Nimmer (1975), "Photocopying and Fair Use" (1977), Seltzer (1977, 1978), Sword (1974–1975), Tseng (1979).

The Four Criteria

Purpose and character of use. According to Judge Ferguson (*Sony,* 1979), the courts have usually used this criterion to determine whether the copyrighted material was used for criticism, research, or another type of independent work. In *Hill* v. *Whalen & Martell* (1914), the court explained: "A copyrighted work is subject to fair criticism, serious or humorous. So far as is necessary to that end, quotations may be made from it" (p. 225).

Judge Kilkenny, in writing the Ninth Circuit's reversal of Ferguson's *Sony* decision, pointed out that this factor is not a commercial versus noncommercial use situation but rather, a commercial versus nonprofit educational purpose situation. (The actual statutory language uses the word *including.* As mentioned earlier, the Act defines *including* to mean *for example.*) While the Ninth Circuit's explanation appears to be a stricter construction of the statute, it is amply supported by case law. For example, in *Triangle* v. *Knight-Ridder* (1978), Judge King commented that the defendant's purpose in using the copyrighted work is the first factor to be examined. He then observed that the importance of permitting nonprofit educational institutions to utilize portions of copyrighted materials and the media's perceived need to disseminate criticism of a work served as catalysts for the development of the judicial doctrine of fair use.*

A fair use defense was denied the defendant in *Henry Holt* v. *Liggett and Myers Tobacco* (1938) because the defendant's pamphlet was neither a scientific treatise nor other type of work designed to advance knowledge. Its purpose was purely commercial in nature. Similarly, in *Loew's* v. *CBS* (1956), the court looked at whether *Autolight,* Jack Benny's burlesque of *Gaslight,* was commercial in nature or in the interests of advancing learning. And, in *Rubin* v. *Boston Magazine Co.* (1981), the court noted that the defendants did not use the copyrighted work for criticism, comment, or news reporting but for commercial purposes. The Second Circuit, in *Meeropol* v. *Nizer* (1977), also looked at whether the alleged infringement was a scholarly or commercial exploitation. This same circuit, in *Rosemont* (1966), indicated that fair use is not restricted to "scholarly works written and prepared for scholarly audiences" (p. 719); in other words, popular works may also be included under fair use as the occasion warrants.

*King's assertion that the needs of educational institutions influenced fair use development is true of the 1976 Act, but this was not a major factor in the early case law involving fair use.

Thus, the courts seem to favor fair use for scholarly and educational purposes, but, as the discussion of *Macmillan* v. *King* (1914) and *Wihtol* v. *Crow* (1962) will show, the application of this criterion is greatly affected by the other fair use factors, especially amount taken and economic harm.

Looking at this factor from a different perspective, Kilkenny (*Sony*, 1981) dismissed as "wholly without merit" First Amendment arguments of increased access to copyrighted works in support of Betamax users, a point of view supported by *Dallas Cowboys Cheerleaders* v. *Scoreboard Posters* (1979), *Sid & Marty Krofft* v. *McDonald's* (1977), and *Walt Disney Productions* v. *Air Pirates* (1978).

Nature of the copyrighted work. Neither case law nor legislative history seems to deal with this factor. Fried (1977) noted that the nature of the copyrighted work is a secondary factor, and Hayes (1978) found that this is the least used factor in deciding fair use.

Informational types of works seem to enjoy a broader scope of fair use protection than those more creative in nature. In other words, a claim of fair use is less likely to be accepted for works categorized as entertainment. However, the shows most likely to be taped off the air are those categorized as entertainment.

The court in *Rosemont* (1966) defined this criterion as whether the distribution of the materials "would serve the public interest in the free dissemination of information" (p. 719). Similarly, in *Time* v. *Bernard Geis* (1968), the court declared that "there is a public interest in having the fullest information available" (p. 675). As a consequence, works in science, law, medicine, history, and biography are usually allowed "some use of prior materials dealing with the same subject matter" (*Rosemont*, 1966, p. 719).

Hart (1981) suggested that the nature of the copyrighted work is also associated with its "availability to the user through normal channels" (p. 347). In other words, if a work is unavailable for purchase, there may be more justification for fair use copying, especially in the context of video recording. However, the question of the potential availability of shows in prepackaged cassettes may mean a more limited approach to fair use copying. This last idea seems true in light of the court's decision in *Meeropol* (1977).

Amount and substantiality of the portion used. One approach the courts take when applying this criterion centers on the idea of a "substantial taking." In *Ager* v. *Peninsular and Oriental Steam*

Navigation Company (1884), the court held that reproducing multiple copies of a substantial amount of a copyrighted work is as much an infringement as reproducing multiple copies of the whole work. The court in *Walt Disney* v. *Air Pirates* (1978) explained: "While other factors in the fair use calculus may not be sufficient by themselves to preclude the fair use defense, this and other courts have accepted the traditional American rule that excessive copying precludes fair use" (p. 776). This notion of excessive or substantial taking is also discussed by the courts in, for example, *Berlin* v. *E. C. Publications* (1964), *Blumcraft of Pittsburgh* v. *Newman Brothers, Inc.* (1968), *Loew's* v. *CBS* (1958), *McGraw-Hill* v. *Worth Publishers* (1971), *Macmillan* v. *King* (1914), *Nichols* v. *Universal Pictures* (1931), *Rosemont* v. *Random House* (1967), *Toksvig* v. *Bruce* (1950), and *Wihtol* v. *Crow* (1962).

Leon v. *Pacific Telephone and Telegraph Company* (1937) is usually cited as the source of the concept that the copying of the whole is not fair use: "Counsel have not disclosed a single authority, nor have we been able to find one, which lends any support to the proposition that wholesale copying and publication of copyrighted material can ever be fair use" (p. 239). The interpretation of this decision played a part in the *Williams & Wilkins* (1975) discussions. The lower court's decision in 1972, referring to *Leon* (1937) and *Wihtol* v. *Crow* (1962), noted that wholesale copying of a copyrighted work is never fair use even if done to further educational or artistic goals and nonprofit in intent. But in reversing this decision, the court of claims (1973) characterized the suggestion that the copying of an entire copyrighted work is never fair use as an overboard generalization, unsupported by case law and contrary to accepted practice. In a footnote, the court explained that *Leon* involved the actual publication and distribution of many copies, not a single copy for personal use, hence its rejection of *Leon* as precedence. Furthermore, the court continued: "There is, in short, no inflexible rule excluding an entire copyrighted work from the area of 'fair use.' Instead, the extent of the copying is one important factor, but only one, to be taken into account, along with several others" (p. 55).

However, Chief Judge Cowan, one of those dissenting in the court of claims decision, asserted that he did not know of any cases that recognized a nonprofit, unauthorized reproduction as a fair use; in fact, case law seemed to indicate the opposite. Lee and Laterza (1977) noted that one result of this new interpretation is that the traditional substantial taking analysis has been discredited by the finding of fair use for verbatim copying under certain circumstances. Hart (1981), though, explained that while substantial taking is the *sine qua non* of infringement, it is not synonymous with infringement. That is, if substantial taking occurs but is considered a fair use, then no infringement has taken place.

According to Seltzer (1977), the reason for the courts' contradictions is that, until *Williams & Wilkins* (1972, 1973, 1975), fair use cases were not a matter of reproducing a copyrighted work for its intrinsic use. Prior case law dealt with a second author's use of the first author's work. In addition, no one had questioned hand copying for private use by scholars, writers, students, and teachers. Thus, part of the conceptual confusion is the apparent conflict between traditionally allowed private use copying and intrinsic use copying exemplified by photocopying. These contradictions, for example, whether or not copying an entire work is a fair use, hold true for off-air taping as well.

Excessive copying, however, is not the courts' sole concern when applying this fair use criterion. Another legacy of Story's *Folsom* (1841) decision is a more qualitative view of fair use: "It is certainly not necessary, to constitute an invasion of copyright, that the whole of a work should be copied, or even a large portion of it, in form or in substance" (p. 348). In other words, copying a small but critical portion of a copyrighted work could be considered an infringement (see, for example, *Bradbury* v. *CBS*, 1961; *Henry Holt* v. *Liggett and Myers Tobacco*, 1938; and *Miller Brewing Company* v. *Carling O'Keafe Breweries of Canada*, 1978).

Effect ... upon the potential market. Hayes's (1978) conclusion that the third criterion is the most important to the contrary, this last factor was consistently indicated by most legal commentators and courts as *the* major consideration. There seems to be general agreement among the courts that a copyright owner has been injured if so much is used that the original work loses value (*Bradbury*, 1961; *Folsom*, 1841; *Hill*, 1914).

Interference with the sale of a copyrighted work is a key factor in deciding whether a use is a fair one. Fair use is generally recognized when the subsequent use of a copyrighted work neither competes with nor otherwise diminishes the value of the original work. And there is no need to prove that the questioned use commercially benefited the copyrighted work as long as it did not harm the original's sales and market. This consideration of possible unfair competition in the market place is voiced in such cases as *Berlin* v. *E. C. Publications* (1964), *College Entrance Book Company, Inc.* v. *Amsco Book Company, Inc.* (1941), *Italian Book*

Corp. v. *ABC* (1978), *Loew's* v. *CBS* (1958), *McGraw-Hill* v. *Worth* (1971), *Meredith* v. *Harper & Row* (1974), *Mura* v. *Columbia Broadcasting System* (1965), *Time* v. *Bernard Geis* (1968), and *Williams & Wilkins* (1975).

In a related approach, the Cambridge Research Institute (1973) noted that the fair use defense was usually sustained when the subsequent work performed a function completely different from that of the copyrighted one. For example, in *Bruzzone* v. *Miller Brewing Co.* (1979), five to six frames of various copyrighted TV advertisements were used in marketing research by the plaintiff. The court held that Bruzzone's use was a fair one. Other cases where a different function had been found a fair use included *Columbia Pictures* v. *National Broadcasting Company* (1955) and *Karll* v. *Curtis Publishing* (1941).

However, in *Loew's* v. *CBS* (1958), the court found that using a copyrighted work for a different function does not automatically allow unreasonable use of it; that is, the amount and substantiality criterion cannot be ignored. In *Metro-Goldwyn-Mayer, Inc.* v. *Showcase Atlanta Cooperative Productions, Inc.* (1979), the court noted that in determining effect on a potential market a comparison must be made not only of the media, but of the works' functions regardless of media. In other words, using Nimmer's (1981) "functional test," if the copies serve the same function as the original, fair use is probably not available as a defense.

This seems supported by *Elektra Records Company* v. *Gem Electronic Distributors, Inc.* (1973). Here the court distinguished between "Make-A-Tape," a coin-operated audiotape duplicating system, and a coin-operated photocopier in, for example, a library:

> (1) Use of a photocopier generally involves duplication of only a portion of a given book or other copyable matter. The Make-A-Tape system duplicates an entire tape, not just part of it. (2) Ordinarily a photocopier would not be used to reproduce an entire book because of the time entailed and a cost in excess of the price of the book. The Make-A-Tape system results in a duplicated tape in less than two minutes and at less cost than the original. (3) The photocopied item is a copy different in form from the original and hence less desirable. The duplicated tape is a true copy essentially identical and equally desirable. (p. 619)

The future market value of a copyrighted work was also included under this criterion. In *Meeropol* v. *Nizer* (1977), the circuit court denied fair use claims because the fact that the Rosenberg letters had been out of print for 20 years did not necessarily mean that some future market could not be injured. Conversely, in *Williams & Wilkins* (1975), criticism of the initial decision's reversal and the later affirmation of the reversal by the Supreme Court centered on the fact that the question of the effect of wholesale copying on the potential market was not addressed.

The *Williams & Wilkins* (1973, 1975) courts were also criticized for deciding in favor of the defendent because the plaintiff had failed to prove actual damages resulting from the alleged infringement, that is, for putting the burden of proof on the plaintiff. Similar criticisms were made of the lower court's decision in *Sony* (1979), especially by the Ninth Circuit Court, which reversed the decision in 1981. According to Nimmer (1975), fair use should never be determined by an inability to prove damages. For example, in *Hill* v. *Whalen & Martell* (1914),

> the court did not require plaintiff to *prove* that defendant's use *actually* reduced the demand for plaintiff's copyrighted work. The court did not discuss any *evidence* of adverse market impact, contenting itself instead to speculate about the probable effects of the defendant's use. This is typical of traditional fair use analysis. ("Photocopying and Fair Use," 1977, pp. 862–863; see also Freid, 1977, for a discussion of the probable effects test)

Thus, while there is agreement on what constitutes economic harm, the courts are not always consistent in their requirements for proof of harmful effect.

The Tale of Two Teachers

Until the 1976 Act and its much publicized guidelines for educators, teachers felt free to reproduce and distribute copyrighted materials to students under the protection of fair use. Litigation was almost nonexistent, perhaps due to the inpracticability of litigating each case or perhaps due to a desire to keep publisher–educator relations on a even keel. With *Williams & Wilkins* (1972, 1973, 1975), however, this situation began to change.

There have been only two cases involving individual teachers and copyright proprietors: *Macmillan* v. *King* (1914) and *Wihtol* v. *Crow* (1962). Although the courts had defined the purpose of use criterion in terms of nonprofit educational purposes as furthering the advancement of knowledge, the teachers *lost* in both cases. The cases, therefore, "appear somewhat anomalous in the development of the fair use doctrine *vis-à-vis* education" (Lee & Laterza, 1977, p. 135).

Macmillan v. *King* (*1914*). The defendant, Melaim Lenoir King, allegedly infringed the copyright of F. W. Taussig's two-volume *Principles of Economics,* published in 1911 by the plaintiff, Macmillan Company, by printing, publishing, leasing, or selling unauthorized, unfair, and unlawful abridgements of the book. King claimed there was no infringement because he was an economics teacher and his use was a customary educational one. True, he used Taussig's text, but it was sold as a textbook to the students and they did indeed buy it. Students came to him for tutoring and aid on a regular basis. Before each session he prepared a brief, one-page outline of the key points for the day's discussion. All such sheets were collected and destroyed; there was no additional charge.

The court distinguished between outlines that merely referred to a book for a particular topic, conveying little actual information about what the book says (and therefore might appropriately be considered study aids without substantial reproduction), and the defendent's method, which

> resulted in an appropriation by him of the author's ideas and language more extensive than the copyright law permits. . . . [For] the copyright protects every substantial component part of the book, as well as the whole. Though the reproduction of the author's ideas and language is incomplete and fragmentary . . . important portions of them are left substantially recognizable. (pp. 866–867)

The defendant's outlines were therefore considered an illegal abridgement of the book. Furthermore, to be considered a publication, it was not necessary for the outlines to have been offered for general sale. The judge concluded:

> I am unable to believe that the defendant's use of the outlines is any less infringement of the copyright because he is a teacher, because he uses them in teaching the contents of the book, because he might lecture upon the contents of the book without infringing, or because his pupils might have taken their own notes of his lectures without infringing. (p. 867)

In addition,

> the evidence can hardly be said to show that the infringing outlines have injured the sale of the book. Nothing more appears than that they might do so by enabling students to get along without the

book who otherwise would have had to buy it. (p. 867; see discussion earlier of economic harm)

Wihtol v. Crow (1962). Tried in 1961 by the district court, judgment was for the defendants Nelson E. Crow, the First Methodist Church of Clarinda (Iowa), and the Clarinda Iowa School District. In 1962, this decision was reversed by the Eighth Circuit. Nimmer was legal counsel for plaintiff in both instances.

Wihtol had published and copyrighted the song "My God and I" in 1935, with an extended copyright following in 1944. Crow, the head of the Clarinda Junior College and High School vocal departments during the 1958–59 school year, found 25 copies of the copyrighted, published version of the song on file in the school library. However, as he found the published version impractical for the average choir, he made a new arrangement and duplicated approximately 48 copies. This new arrangement was performed once by the high school choir of 84 voices at one of the regular monthly chapel services and twice on one Sunday by the church's choir.

In early June 1959, Crow wrote Wihtol about the new arrangement, asking if the company was interested. Wihtol requested a copy for perusal. In late July, Wihtol informed Crow (1) that his arrangement was a copyright infringement; (2) that since he had not sent the requested copy, an investigation had been made; (3) that a $250 payment had to be made within 90 days; and (4) that all copies of the new arrangement had to be sent to the firm. On September 1, 1959, Crow sent the copies to Wihtol; on January 15, 1960, Wihtol commenced legal action. Of course, both the school district and church denied that Crow was their agent.

According to the district court, the crucial issue was

> whether the sum total of defendant Crow's actions in experimenting with the copyrighted song . . . constituted such unfair use of plaintiffs' [sic] copyrighted work as to amount to an infringement thereof. The Court finds that there was no infringement, that Crow's activity remained within the realm of fair use of plaintiff's work and did not constitute an infringement. (p. 393)

The court explained that Crow's use of the song was only an experiment with a new arrangement. It also viewed Wihtol's letter to Crow as smacking of extortion and therefore not entitled to relief. Thus, it dismissed the plaintiff's complaint.

However, Wihtol appealed the decision and won a reversal, where the Eighth Circuit Court asserted that "whatever may be the breadth of the doctrine of 'fair use,' it is not conceivable to us that the copying of all, or substantially all, of a copyrighted song can be held to be a 'fair use' merely because the infringer had no intent to infringe" (p. 387). Therefore, it held:

> (1) that . . . Crow is an infringer . . . ; (2) that the Church, as his employer, is jointly liable with him under the doctrine of respondent superior; (3) that the School District is entitled to dismissal, for want of jurisdiction, of the action against it [but compare this last point with *Mills Music* v. *Arizona* (1979)]. (p. 389)

There are two interesting side notes to this case. First, the current "Guidelines for Educational Uses of Music" (H. R. 94-1476) include the following provision: "Printed copies which have been purchased may be edited or simplified provided that the fundamental character of the work is not distorted or the lyrics, if any, altered or lyrics added if none exist" (p. 71). The other item of interest is that Blackmun was one of the circuit judges for the *Wihtol* case. Thirteen years later, he was one of the U.S. Supreme Court justices before whom *Williams & Wilkins* (1975) was heard. Blackmun, however, took no part in this decision; hence its affirmation by an equally divided court. Considering that the *Wihtol* reversal was a unanimous circuit court decision, there is speculation that Blackmun would have voted in favor of Williams & Wilkins, thereby possibly altering the current state of fair use photocopying. This theory is further supported by Blackmun's stance on the Supreme Court's *Sony* (1984) decision. He was one of the four judges who voted against home off-air taping and actually wrote the dissenting opinion. (See the discussion of Blackmun's comments later in this chapter.)

Off-Air Videotaping and Related Cases

Since the new Act rendered *Columbia Broadcasting System* v. *Vanderbilt University* (1976) moot, there have apparently been no cases dealing with fair use, off-air taping, and an individual educational institution. Nor have any suits been brought against an individual faculty member. It is difficult, therefore, to ascertain how the courts would rule if faced with such an issue – not that they have necessarily shown consistency in applying fair use criteria.

There have been, however, five decisions that may shed some light on the issue. The most important is *Encyclopaedia Britannica Educational Corporation* v. *Crooks* (1978, 1982, 1983) – commonly called *BOCES* – a *cause célèbre* in educational circles that focused on large-scale, systematic off-air taping activities by an educational consortium. Despite the hullabaloo, the *Sony* (1979, 1981, 1984) decision does not address educational off-air taping. It centers on home off-air taping and excludes – as specified by the court – tape duplication, copying from pay television, and off-air taping by individuals or groups for use outside the home. However, the courts' discussions of fair use and off-air taping merit consideration. Three other cases that bear relation to judicial thinking on TV broadcasts are *Walt Disney Productions* v. *Alaska Television Network* (1969), *Fortnightly Corporation* v. *United Artists Television* (1968), and *Teleprompter* v. *CBS* (1974).

BOCES (1978, 1982, 1983). The plaintiffs were Encyclopaedia Britannica Educational Corporation, Learning Corporation of America, and Time-Life Films – three corporations that produce, acquire, and license educational motion pictures. The defendants, such as C. N. Crooks, were all staff of the Board of Cooperative Educational Services (BOCES), First Supervisory District, Erie County, New York. BOCES, itself named a defendant, is "a nonprofit corporation organized under the Education Law to provide educational services to the public schools in Erie County" (p. 282). It originally encompassed 21 districts for a total of over 100 schools; in 1982, it had 19 districts (some had combined) with approximately the same number of schools.

The original decision (1978) by District Judge Curtin was on a motion for a preliminary injunction against the defendants for copyright infringement. The motion was granted. The next decision came after a nonjury trial and granted the plaintiffs a permanent injunction (1982). The latest decision (1983) dealt with damages and whether BOCES could make some temporary off-air recordings. Each will be discussed below.

The original complaint alleged that BOCES videotaped, without permission, a number of the plaintiffs' copyrighted films and distributed copies to the school districts for delayed viewing by the students. The plaintiffs sought, therefore, to

> enjoin the defendants from videotaping plaintiffs' copyrighted motion pictures from television broadcasts, recopying the videotapes, distributing these tapes to the school districts, displaying the copies in classrooms, and transmitting the videotaped films to the schools over closed-circuit television cables. (p. 282)

BOCES began its service of off-air taping of educational programs in 1966; by 1968, a catalog was openly available. The service was staffed by five to eight full-time workers with videotape equipment estimated to be worth $500,000. Between 1976 and 1977 alone, it provided duplication of 10,000 videotapes. BOCES would make master videotapes of entire films, the majority of which were shown on the local PBS channel with some from commercial stations. A school would request in writing a particular show and provide a blank tape. BOCES would then make a copy from its master tape at cost to the school with no charge to the students. BOCES would hold a master copy for varying periods before erasure; the schools usually reused their tapes and thus erased previous programs. However, returning a tape for erasure was not required, nor did BOCES monitor the actual use of a tape. It was simply assumed the use was educational. Also, no record was kept of how often a tape was shown in the classroom, nor of what actually happened to the tape afterward.

BOCES claimed that this videotape service was a significant component of the instructional support services it provided and was

> relied upon by the teachers in planning their school curricula. Since many of the programs are televised when classes are not in session or at times that do not coincide with coverage of the subject in a particular course of study, it is claimed that the students cannot view these programs unless videotapes are available. . . . If the program is discontinued, public education would be greatly disrupted. (p. 282)

While admitting to videotaping the plaintiffs' copyrighted films without paying license fees or obtaining permission, BOCES opposed the preliminary injunction motion on three grounds. The first was fair use: "Noncommercial videotaping of television programs off the air for purposes of delayed viewing in the classroom is not a copyright infringement" (p. 283). The second was on the grounds that laches and estoppel barred preliminary relief. The third was that "any presumption of irreparable harm is rebutted by the existence of a clear measure of damage provided by the plaintiffs' licensing agreements, coupled with BOCES's records of the number of copies it has produced" (p. 283). A fourth defense was added in post-argument papers:

> Most of the television programs videotaped . . . were purchased by the local educational channel, WNED-TV, with state funds. . . . these appropriations were made to WNED for the purpose of providing instructional broadcasts for the public schools at no cost to

the schools. . . . the plaintiffs are seeking to force the state to pay twice for the use of their films . . . the appropriations would not have been made if the instructional programs could not be utilized by the schools through videotaping. (p. 283)

In granting the preliminary injunction, Judge Curtin pointed out that a "motion for preliminary relief should be granted only upon a clear showing of either probable success on the merits and possible irreparable injury or sufficiently serious questions going to the merits to make them a fair ground for litigation" (p. 283). However, he noted that the standard was less rigorous when copyright infringement was the issue because it may be presumed that the copyright holder suffered irreparable harm when the exclusivity of the copyright was invaded. Therefore, "the plaintiff in a copyright case is entitled to a preliminary injunction even without a detailed showing of irreparable harm if the plaintiff demonstrates probable success on the merits of a prima facie case of infringement" (p. 283).

Looking first at the question of irreparable injury, Curtin found the plaintiffs' showing of harm sufficiently detailed for the purposes of the injunction. Furthermore, he said that if the plaintiffs' allegation that BOCES's practices substantially threaten their educational film market was true, then the injury extended beyond lost licensing fees into areas not readily reduced to monetary terms.

Moreover, BOCES does not keep records of the number of times each film is displayed in the schools, and it does not guarantee return of the videotapes. Absent such records and guarantees, the licensing agreements would not provide a clear measure of damages caused by distributing copies of the films to the schools. (p. 284)

Turning to the issue of probable success on the merits, Curtin first explained the problem involved and indicated that a legislative – not judicial – decision was more appropriate.

Educational institutions have been videotaping television broadcasts for strictly educational purposes for some time. The legality of such copying has never been determined, either by the courts* or by the legislature. The problem of accommodating the competing

*Curtin footnoted *Walt Disney* v. *Alaska Television Network* (discussed later) as not in point because it dealt with commercial, for-profit videotaping with no question of fair use involved.

interests of both educators and film producers raises major policy questions which the legislature is better equipped to resolve. However, Congress has not as yet provided a legislative solution to the problem, but has left the issue to the courts. (p. 284)

According to the judge, the key factor to be weighed in determining probable success on the merits was fair use. Without fair use, which "must be considered in determining the existence of a prima facie case for purposes of preliminary relief" (p. 285), Curtin stated the "BOCES' videotaping activities would seem to constitute a blatant violation of the plaintiffs' exclusive rights to copy and perform their films" (p. 285).

Curtin's discussion of fair use centered on the Section 107 criteria, which he applied to his analysis of BOCES' use of *Williams & Wilkins* (1973, 1975) as support for its fair use stance.* In terms of the purpose and character of use, he found similarities for "both sets of defendants have been providing services on a strictly noncommercial basis to a limited class of requesters for the purpose of promoting two traditionally favored areas of endeavor: science and education" (p. 286). However, the similarity did not extend to the substantiality and marketplace effect criteria. In *Williams & Wilkins,* a single article, 50 pages or less, from a periodical was involved, while in *BOCES* an entire film had been copied. When copying an entire film, "the potential impact of the copyright owner's market is much greater because the reproduction is interchangeable with the original" (p. 286). In *Williams & Wilkins,* medical research would have been injured by a finding of infringement, but BOCES could continue its service through licensing agreements pending final resolution of the case. In *Williams & Wilkins,* the decision that the market effect had been minimal came after a full trial. In *BOCES,* there had been no trial as yet as the motion was for a preliminary injunction. However, for the purposes of determining probable success on the merits, Curtin decided the issue of economic loss in favor of the plaintiffs. He also questioned BOCES's claim of fair use given the scope of its off-air taping activities: "This case does not involve an isolated instance of a teacher copying copyrighted material for classroom use but concerns a highly organized and systematic program for reproducing videotapes on a massive scale" (p. 287).

As for BOCES's post-argument paper regarding funding for WNED to broadcast the films as sufficient payment without additional payments for licenses, Curtin recommended that it be devel-

BOCES itself was actually under the 1909 Act.

oped as a possible defense at the trial. Laches was dismissed based on a timetable that included attempts at out-of-court settlements and the magnitude of the planning involved in such a lawsuit. Curtin concluded: "Considering all of these factors, I find that the plaintiffs have established a prima facie case entitling them to preliminary relief" (p. 287).

Although granting the preliminary injunction, Curtin recognized that such an order might disrupt the educational process. He recommended that BOCES obtain licenses from the plaintiffs as a means of overcoming this difficulty. In addition, he allowed BOCES to continue its distribution of materials already taped and incorporated into the schools' curricula on the condition that a plan to monitor the use of tapes and require their return and erasure within a specified time was implemented. Furthermore, he directed the concerned parties to meet with him a few days later in order to frame guidelines for complying with his decision.

The guidelines developed to implement the preliminary injunction included in an appendix to the 1979 subcommittee hearings on educational off-air taping. Seven provisions were agreed upon:

1. Records were to be kept of the number of copies made from each master tape, the date each was made, the name of the requesting school, the date it was delivered to the school, the date it was returned, and the date it was erased.
2. Receipts signed by the receiving school and data on the number of showings, their date and time, the audience, and its size were to be collected by a designated BOCES employee.
3. The records and receipts so gathered were to be filed with both the court and the plaintiffs' attorneys.
4. Schools were to return their copy of a tape within 30 days. The same employee who collected the data required in no. 2 above was responsible for ensuring the return of the film within the specified time. Failure to return the film within 45 days was to be reported to the court and to the plaintiffs' attorneys.
5. Prompt erasure of each copy after its return to BOCES was required.
6. BOCES was allowed to determine whether a film had been incorporated into the school curricula.
7. Each participating school was to receive a copy of this order.

Curtin explained that the purpose of these monitoring provisions was to establish concise data enabling the plaintiffs to measure their damages should they ultimately prevail in this action. At the same time, these provisions prevented the disruption of ex-

isting BOCES services to the schools. In conclusion, Curtin once
again authorized BOCES to enter licensing agreements with the
plaintiffs.

In the fall of 1980, a nonjury trial involving 17 witnesses and 87
exhibits was held. District Judge Curtin once again presided. At
stake was whether the preliminary injunction granted in 1978
would become permanent. While the central question still focused
on whether an educational cooperative's large-scale, systematic
off-air videorecording of copyrighted works was fair use, the trial
concerned itself only with the use of 19 specific films copyrighted
by the plaintiffs. Almost two years passed before Curtin announced his decision on July 21, 1982. In keeping with his earlier
decision, Curtin granted the plaintiffs a permanent injunction prohibiting BOCES from copying their copyrighted works.

The plaintiffs' argument basically remained unchanged from
that used at the time the preliminary injunction was sought. The
defendants' position, however, had undergone some refinement.
This time, the defendants' legal contentions were that technological change had rendered the Copyright Act ambiguous, that fair
use was applicable, and that under the 1909 Act BOCES was a
"transmitting organization" and under the 1976 Act a "broadcasting entity." In addition, BOCES claimed First Amendment protection because educational access to information is in the public
interest and the doctrine of estoppel barred any action. The defendants concluded their legal contentions by saying that even if
they had infringed, they should be responsible only for actual
damages, since future harm was too speculative.

Turning first to the issue of fair use, Curtin noted that its application to the *BOCES* case was basically discussed when the preliminary injunction was granted. This trial essentially confirmed
Curtin's earlier opinion. However, some additional facts were
raised, and he addressed these in this discussion. First, both sides
cited the *Sony* decisions as support for their arguments. In *Sony*
(1979), there had been an attempt to cite *BOCES* (1978) as a similar case. Judge Ferguson had rejected this reasoning (see discussion following). Here Curtin supported Ferguson's statement
because he thought that off-air taping for educational classroom
use was a different issue than off-air taping for home use. Second,
although *BOCES* was primarily under the 1909 Act, Curtin used
the Section 107 criteria in his discussion of fair use. He did so because the Section 107 criteria are illustrative, not exhaustive.
Also, Congress did not change the doctrine of fair use; a case-by-
case examination is still necessary.

As might have been expected, Curtin began his criteria analysis with a discussion of the fourth criterion – harm. According to Curtin, this criterion focuses on diminishing or prejudicing potential sales, interfering with the marketability of a copyrighted work, fulfilling the same function as the original, and the *cumulative* effect of mass reproduction. The plaintiffs claimed BOCES's copying harmed the market and potential videotape sales market. Time-Life prefers to sell and duplicate its own copies to schools; both Learning Corporation of America and Encyclopaedia Britannica Educational Corporation have various licensing arrangements. All agreed that if BOCES could freely copy their programs off the air, then these arrangements would be meaningless and worthless.

Of the 19 works in question, BOCES owned 16 in film format. The plaintiffs said that by copying and loaning the films in videotape format, BOCES was directly interfering with the marketing of the works. In addition, another work, which eventually was bought in film format, might have been purchased earlier if a videotape copy had not been available. This was seen as prejudicing the potential market from a cumulative perspective. Further diminishing and prejudicing potential sales was the BOCES policy of purchasing an additional copy of a film for every 30 or more videotape requests it received for a title. Judge Curtin concluded, "Fair use must be reasonable. . . . Plaintiffs' choice of facing unlimited videotape copying or abandonment of the educational television market cannot be seen as providing reasonable market alternatives to fair use by the defendants" (p. 711).

Purpose and character of use were next discussed. While the nonprofit, educational usage of the copyrighted works was not really questioned, this alone does not automatically sanction fair use. Curtin noted that H.R. 94-1476 said that nonprofit educational use should be weighed *along with* other factors. In other words, by itself it is not conclusive of fair use. Furthermore, reiterating his earlier comment that fair use is based upon reasonableness, Curtin remarked that the sheer scope and sophistication of BOCES's videotaping production, duplication, and distribution could not be deemed reasonable under fair use. In addition, since BOCES already owned 16 of the 19 works in film format, the time-shifting argument for classroom access lost importance and validity. And since an annual program schedule with descriptions of the shows and their recording rights was available, educational access was promoted while the plaintiffs' rights were protected. In other words, the plaintiffs' various licensing agreements were seen as a solution for reconciling educational access and technological change with plaintiffs' need for protection.

The next criterion discussed was the nature of the copyrighted work. As with the previous two criteria, Curtin concluded that educational content cannot be used to justify extensive, systematic copying as being in the public interest. He also pointed out that this case, unlike *Williams & Wilkins* (1973), did not deal with out-of-print, unavailable materials that contained important information. All 19 of the films in question were available from the plaintiffs.

Substantiality, the last criterion discussed, received a similar analysis. Although Curtin observed that the more copied, the less likely was a fair use finding, he rejected the plaintiffs' claim that off-air taping can never be fair use. One source he cited for this rejection was H.R. 94-1476, which said that off-air taping may, in specific instances, be fair use. He also maintained his preliminary injunction finding that *Williams & Wilkins* did not match the circumstances under consideration in this case. In addition, BOCES's having kept and used some tapes for 10 years was seen as a virtual substitution for purchase and/or licensing and, therefore, could not be considered fair use. Curtin also remarked that whether the criteria had to be considered individually or together was irrelevant to the issue since harm had been amply demonstrated.

Curtin also decided that BOCES's practices were not protected by the First Amendment or the doctrine of estoppel. In fact, BOCES's failure to inquire about copying authorization in light of the copyright notice on the works precluded estoppel. Related to the First Amendment argument were the contentions dealing with TV broadcasts over public airwaves and broadcasts on public TV paid for with public funds. Curtin dismissed these as "farfetched" and "erroneous."

> The court can find no constitutional impediment in the licensing of plaintiffs' works for television broadcast, the use of public television stations to transmit these broadcasts, and the protection of plaintiffs' copyrighted works under the law.... The plaintiffs' choice of media or the source of funding used for purchasing broadcast licenses does not abrogate their rights as copyright holders. (p. 176)

Curtin also said that the issue of whether BOCES was a transmitting or broadcasting entity was without merit; that would not have given BOCES the right to reproduce and distribute taped copies.

Thus, in this second decision, Curtin concluded that BOCES was not protected by fair use or fair use considerations, not insulated by the estoppel doctrine. A permanent injunction was therefore granted to prohibit the copying of the plaintiffs' works. However, Curtin did not award attorneys' fees to the plaintiffs because the case dealt with "novel, unsettled, or complex problems" for which the courts generally do not award such fees. He also did not order the immediate erasure of BOCES's entire library. Instead, he suggested purchasing negotiations or other suitable arrangements so that the existing library would not be wasted. If no agreement could be reached, the plaintiffs could then ask that the infringing copies be erased.

On March 10, 1983, Judge Curtin handed down the third of his *BOCES* decisions. This decision centered on three remaining issues: (1) the defendants' motion to be allowed some temporary off-air taping of plaintiffs' works; (2) the plaintiffs' motion for an award of attorneys' fees; and (3) issues involving damages and the number and types of infringements committed by BOCES.

The temporary use issue stemmed from Curtin's 1982 permanent injunction prohibiting future copying, in which he had observed that some limited or temporary use might be considered fair use under the 1976 Act. The defendants were therefore requesting that the injunction be amended to allow for such use. In examining the defendants' motion, Curtin looked to H.R. 94-1476 and noted the guidelines later issued. He also reexamined Section 107 fair use criteria in light of this request. Beginning once again with the last criterion, harm, he returned to the ideas of licensing and diminishing potential sales. Curtin said that it was significant that all the plaintiffs' works were available for rental or lease for short (as short as one to three days) or long-term periods. He also referred to his 1982 decision's discussion of licensing agreements. He therefore concluded that BOCES's taping would interfere with the marketability of these works and that the cumulative effect of temporary taping "would tend to diminish or prejudice the potential short-term lease or rental market for these works" (p. 1251).

According to Curtin, this availability factor is also important when looking at the nature of the copyrighted work. Again referring to his 1982 decision, Curtin said that if a work was unavailable through normal channels, there would be more justification for copying. However, in this case, the works can be supplied by the plaintiffs and, thus, substantiality is not in favor of the defendants.

As for the purpose and character of use, while education is a laudable objective, the specific purpose is time-shifting. Time-shifting is more convenient for the defendants, but, as Curtin noted in his 1982 decision, fair use is based on reasonableness, and this does not inherently include convenience. Furthermore, S. 94-473 indicated that off-air taping for convenience was not fair use. Curtin therefore concluded that since the works were available, temporary or limited time uses were not reasonable. But, he added: "The court's finding that defendants' request for temporary use is not fair use of plaintiffs' works is intended only to affect the parties in this case and is based solely on the law and the facts as presented in the instant action" (p. 1251).

Also in keeping with his 1982 decision, Curtin refused to award attorneys' fees. But, since *BOCES* was under the 1909 Act, the plaintiffs were entitled to costs. As for damages, the minimum statutory damage is $250. The plaintiffs sought $250 per copying, vending, and performance infringement committed. Curtin ruled that there was no vending infringement under the 1909 Act but pointed out that this might be different under Section 106(3) of the 1976 Act. He did, however, consider showing the tapes in class a public performance.

Curtin found the defendants liable as contributory infringers, that is, "one who, with knowledge of the infringing activity, induces, causes, or materially contributes to the infringing activity, induces, causes or materially contributes to the infringing conduct of another" (p. 1256). He also noted that a mistake about the legal consequences of one's actions is not an excuse for infringements. Therefore, "all defendants are jointly and severally liable for costs and damages in this action" (p. 1256). Who are these defendants? Mainly BOCES Videotape Service employees and members of BOCES who were ultimately responsible for the videotaping activities. What was the dollar amount of damages and court costs? Damages came to approximately $63,500 and court costs to $15,000. And what about the attorneys' fees for the defense? These ranged in the area of $200,000.

A curious aspect of the *BOCES* decisions is that Curtin's 1982 and 1983 rulings, although consistent with his 1978 preliminary injunction, seem to follow closely the Ninth Circuit's reasoning in its disputed *Sony* (1981) decision, a reasoning upheld in Justice Blackmun's dissenting opinion to the Supreme Court's *Sony* (1984) decision. Thus, despite the courts' stated differences between situations addressed in *BOCES* and *Sony,* the underlying reasoning is similar. How, if at all, this stricter analysis of the fair use criteria will affect off-air taping by individual educational institutions is not yet clear.

Universal City Studios v. *Sony* (*1979, 1981, 1984*). The plaintiffs in this case were Universal Studios and Walt Disney Productions. The defendants included not only Sony, the manufacturer of the Betamax videotape recorder (hence the case is often referred to as the Betamax case), but stores that demonstrated the machine, and even a Betamax owner. The chief issue was whether off-air taping of copyrighted audio-visual materials by Betamax owners in the privacy of their homes for personal, noncommercial use constituted an infringement of copyright. The district court found *no* infringement; on appeal, the circuit court found infringement; and the U.S. Supreme Court supported the district court's finding of no infringement by reversing the circuit court's decision.

Three cases discussed in the original briefs as illustrative of fair use in a noncommercial context were *Williams & Wilkins* (1973, 1975), *Wihtol* (1962), and *BOCES* (1978). District Judge Ferguson (*Sony*, 1979), however, indicated their inappropriateness for the case at hand. *Williams & Wilkins* had little precedential value since the ruling was by a divided court. It was also limited to its unique factual situation. Moreover, the court's treatment of economic harm had been widely criticized. *Wihtol* and *BOCES*, two educational cases, were dismissed as having little precedential value, as the former involved a public performance and the latter involved only an opinion granting preliminary relief. Ferguson noted that in *BOCES* "the court was not conclusively finding infringement but rather only a prima facie case thereof" (p. 679). Furthermore, *BOCES* was "more dissimilar to the situation here than similar" (p. 679) since home off-air taping was not involved. Thus, home and educational off-air videotaping appear to be separate issues, shedding little light on each other. But the Ninth Circuit's discussion of the 1976 Act and fair use merits consideration because of the similarities between its reasoning and that of the *BOCES* court.

Circuit Judge Kilkenny took exception to the lower court's search of legislative history for congressional intent:

> The issue is not whether Congress exhibited an intent to protect a copyright holder from certain reproduction of his works. It had already expressed its intent to do so by extending the "bundle of rights" set forth in ¶106 to copyright owners, *subject to specific sections*, to wit: ¶¶107–118. (*Sony*, 1981, p. D-2)

He also described the much criticized Copyright Act as "unambiguous." According to Kilkenny, Section 108 provided "strong support for the conclusion that Congress was concerned about unauthorized reproduction of audiovisual works, *whether or not such reproductions were for profit*" (p. D-2; emphasis added).

In his discussion of fair use, Kilkenny maintained that

> despite the nebulous character of the doctrine, previous case law and the general copyright scheme do provide us with considerable guidance. . . . It is noteworthy that the statute does not list "convenience" or "entertainment" or "increased access" as purposes within the general scope of fair use. (p. D-4)

Also, the judge pointed out that fair use has not generally been applied where the copy of the copyrighted work was used for the same intrinsic purpose as the original. Two exceptions to this rule were *Williams & Wilkins* (1973, 1975) and the lower court's decision in the case at hand. In addition, Kilkenny observed that "the result of applying fair use to intrinsic use cases like *Williams & Wilkins Co.* and this case is a fundamental restructuring of the copyright system not justified by the statutory scheme or traditional notions of fair use" (p. D-5).

The fourth fair use criterion, economic effect, received the most attention. Kilkenny concurred with the dissenters in *Williams & Wilkins* who objected to the court's conclusion that the plaintiff had failed to prove actual damages. Like them, he complained that this was "too great a burden to impose on copyright plaintiffs" (p. D-6). He supported Nimmer's suggestion that the question should center on whether the "infringing work *tends* to diminish or prejudice the potential sale of plaintiff's work" (p. D-6). The cumulative effect of mass reproduction made possible by videotape recorders was seen as an activity that tended to diminish the potential market. Referring to copyright's purpose of economic incentive, Kilkenny remarked: "It is clear that home users assign economic value to their ability to have control over access to copyrighted works. The copyright laws would seem to require that the copyright owner be given the opportunity to exploit this market" (p. D-6).

Before turning to the Supreme Court's pronouncements on time-shifting and fair use, the petitioners' (Sony Corporation, et al.) and respondents' (Universal City Studios and Walt Disney Productions) discussions of fair use in their 1982 briefs warrant mention. Like the Supreme Court decision itself, these briefs illustrate the dichotomy between users and copyright owners regarding fair use.

The petitioners' brief ("Selected portions," 1982) was supported by 15 amicus briefs, which basically fell into three categories. Ten of the amicus briefs centered on the Ninth Circuit's approach and First Amendment arguments; three, on the effect of restrictions on VTR sales; and two, on the effect of contributory infringement. The petitioners' brief itself focused on Section 107 and the legislative history of the 1976 Act. The petitioners maintained that the lack of a specific exception or limitation was a fair use under Section 107 (but compare Section 107) for several reasons:

1. The purpose and character of such use is to increase access. This is not only consistent with the First Amendment's concern for the fullest information dissemination over the public airwaves, but also with Universal and Disney's concern over the size of their audience. Such taping allows them to reach more viewers.
2. The Ninth Circuit's intrinsic use argument is contrary to the spirit of Section 107 because it tends to freeze the meaning of the section.
3. The nature of the work copied is not always entertainment. All shows can provide thought, comment, and reaction.
4. The district court found no damage to potential markets.

In addition, the brief argued that the legislative history of the 1976 Copyright Act included the 1971 House and Senate reports on sound recordings. The House report indicated that home recording for private use was not limited by the 1971 copyright protection granted. Since the issue was resolved in 1971, there was no need to rediscuss it for the 1976 Act. Another argument was that home VTRs, like cable television in *Fortnightly* (1968) and *Teleprompter* (1974), only enhanced the viewer's capacity to receive a broadcaster's signal.

The brief went on to address the issues of contributory infringement and continuing royalties. The petitioners claimed that even if home off-air taping was found to be an infringement, they were not liable for contributory infringement because a VTR is a staple article of commerce like a camera, Xerox machine, or typewriter. As for compulsory licensing as a judicial remedy for copyright infringement, the petitioners pointed out that there was neither statutory provision nor precedent.

In conclusion, the petitioners observed that Universal and Disney were trying to make this the first U.S. case to find copyright infringement on a copy of something for private, personal use and entirely in the home. The petitioners also charged that Universal and Disney were seeking profits beyond what was in the public interest.

The respondents' brief ("Selected portions," 1982) was supported by six amicus briefs. The six basically dealt with the idea that home off-air taping does not equal fair use. The respondents' brief itself also argued that home off-air taping is not fair use and that the Ninth Circuit's criteria considerations were correct. Fair use, according to the respondents, allows a limited use of previous works in order to create new ones in areas of universal social concern. Home off-air taping does not meet this purpose of a new, independently creative work and, therefore, does not meet the basic justification for fair use. In addition, home off-air taping does not satisfy Section 107 criteria:

1. Home off-air taping is for convenience, *not* for criticism, comment, news reporting, teaching, scholarship, or research.
2. It involves the copying of *entire* works that are entertainment-oriented – not informational – in nature.
3. The unlimited copies thus made serve the same function as and compete with the copyrighted originals.

The brief also claimed that increased access via broadcasts taped off the public airwaves did not override fair use and that the overall scheme and history of the 1976 Act showed that Congress did not intend home taping to be fair use.

The respondents also pointed out that the staple article of commerce doctrine is under patent, not copyright, law. Sony satisfied the test for a contributory infringer because it knew people would tape off the air, thus infringing copyrights. On the issue of compulsory licensing, the respondents suggested that as the district court had not yet considered the remedy question, it would be premature for the Supreme Court to do so. However, they did favor a continuing royalty.

In June 1982, the U.S. Supreme Court agreed to review the case. On January 18, 1983, it heard the arguments. On July 6, 1983, the court ordered a rehearing of the arguments during its October 1983 term but gave no reason. (A case is sometimes reheard if the majority of judges cannot agree on a decision.) Finally, on January 17, 1984, the Supreme Court handed down its five to four decision reversing that of the Ninth Circuit.

Justice Stevens delivered the opinion of the court. Chief Justice Burger and Justices Brennan, White, and O'Connor joined in the opinion. As mentioned earlier, Justice Blackmun wrote the dissenting opinion; joining him were Justices Marshall, Powell, and Rehnquist.

The question actually addressed by the Supreme Court was *not* home off-air taping per se. Rather, the question was whether Sony's sale of the Betamax VTR to the general public violated any of the rights conferred on Universal and Disney by the Copyright Act. In other words, was Sony liable for contributory infringement? To answer this question, the Supreme Court first had to decide such issues as whether home off-air taping was an infringement. The court held that VTR sales to the general public was not contributory infringement.

In its decision, the Supreme Court reviewed those of the district and Ninth Circuit courts. According to the Supreme Court, the district court concluded that noncommercial, home use recording of programs broadcast over the public airwaves was fair use and not an infringement. In reaching this decision, the district court emphasized that (1) the programs were broadcast free to the public; (2) the use was noncommercial in nature; and, (3) time-shifting served the public interest by increasing access to TV programs — access limited not only by inconvenience but by a need to work and the competitiveness of counterprogramming. It also concluded that Sony was not liable for contributory infringement because the Betamax VTR was a staple article of commerce. The district court also concluded that an injunction was inappropriate because the Betamax could be used legally to record noncopyrighted shows and those whose owners, like Fred Rogers of *Mr. Rogers' Neighborhood,* did not object to noncommercial, home taping. An injunction would prevent these noninfringing uses.

The Supreme Court characterized the Ninth Circuit's holding that Universal and Disney were "entitled to enjoin the distribution of VTR's, to collect royalties on the sale of such equipment, or to obtain other relief" as enlarging the scope of Universal and Disney's statutory monopolies to encompass an article of commerce not the subject of copyright. "Such an expansion of the copyright privilege is beyond the limits of the grants authorized by Congress" (p. 4090).

Justice Stevens then expanded on the topic of copyright privilege. He reaffirmed the precedence of public access over economic reward: "The monopoly privileges that Congress may authorize are neither unlimited nor primarily designed to provide a special private benefit. Rather, the limited grant is a means by which an important public purpose may be achieved" (pp. 4092–4093). He also noted the "judiciary's reluctance to expand the protection afforded by the copyright without explicit legislative guidance is a recurring theme" (p. 4093). The Court defers to Congress when major technological innovations alter the market for copyrighted materials because Congress has the "constitutional authority and institutional ability" (p. 4093) to handle the various competing interests involved. Therefore, "in a case like this, in which Congress has not plainly marked our course, we must be circumspect in construing the scope of rights created by a legislative enactment which never contemplated such a calculus of interests" (p. 4093).

According to Stevens, copyright "protection has never accorded the copyright owner complete control over all possible uses of his work" (p. 4093). While Section 106 grants the copyright owner exclusive rights including reproduction, not all reproductions are "within the exclusive domain of the copyright owner; some are in the public domain. Any individual may reproduce a copyrighted work for a 'fair use'; the copyright owner does not possess the exclusive right to such a use" (p. 4094).

The Court next turned to the issue of contributory infringement. Universal and Disney had argued that liability for copyright infringement was established by supplying the "means" for infringing and encouraging it through advertisement. The Court dismissed this argument as a gross generalization, pointing out that Sony does not supply the works and not everything copied is copyrighted or an unauthorized use. If Sony is to be held for vicarious liability, it must rest on the fact it has "sold equipment with constructive knowledge of the fact that . . . [its] customers may use the equipment to make unauthorized copies of copyrighted material" (p. 4094). However, "there is no precedent in the law of copyright for the imposition of vicarious liability on such a theory" (p. 4094). The critical issue, therefore, is whether the Betamax is a staple article of commerce, that is, widely used for legitimate, unobjectionable purposes.

So Stevens examined the question of whether the Betamax is "capable of commercially significant noninfringing uses" (p. 4096). Instead of discussing "how much use is commercially significant," Stevens observed that one potential use satisfies this question: "private, noncommercial time-shifting in the home" (p. 4096). It does so because (1) Universal and Disney have no right to prevent other copyright holders from authorizing it for their programs and (2) the district court found that even unauthorized home time-shifting of programs is legitimate fair use.

According to Stevens, Section 107 of the 1976 Copyright Act

identifies factors that enable the Court to apply an "equitable rule of reason." Two of the four fair use criteria were discussed: the commercial or nonprofit character of the use; and the effect of the use on the potential market. Private, home use time-shifting was considered a noncommercial, nonprofit use.

> Moreover, when one considers the nature of a televised copyrighted audiovisual work . . . and that timeshifting merely enables a viewer to see such a work he had been invited to witness in its entirety free of charge, the fact that the entire work is reproduced . . . does not have its ordinary effect of mitigating against a finding of fair use. (p. 4098)

No harm to the market was found and to prohibit "such noncommercial uses would merely inhibit access to ideas without any countervailing benefit" (p. 4098).

Using the district court's findings, the Court concluded that (1) Sony showed a significant likelihood that many copyright owners who license works for broadcast on free TV do not object to private time-shifting and (2) Universal and Disney failed to demonstrate harmful effects to potential markets by time-shifting. The Betamax, therefore, is capable of substantial noninfringing uses, and Sony's sale of it is not a contributory infringement. In summary:

> One may search the Copyright Act in vain for any sign that the elected representatives of the millions of people who watch television every day have made it unlawful to copy a program for later viewing at home, or have enacted a flat prohibition against the sale of machines that make such copying possible.
>
> It may well be that Congress will take a fresh look at this new technology, just as it so often has examined other innovations in the past. But it is not our job to apply laws that have not yet been written. Applying the copyright statute, as it now reads, to the facts as they have been developed in this case, the judgment of the Court of Appeals must be reversed. (p. 4100)

Justice Blackmun's well-reasoned dissenting opinion is included here for two reasons. First, his sharp criticisms of the majority opinion are a forerunner of those sure to follow this decision. Second, his support of the Ninth Circuit's reasoning and decision resurrects echoes of Curtin's *BOCES* decisions.

Blackmun considered the Court had belittled Universal and Disney's position by characterizing it as "unprecedented" and

"novel." He disagreed with the Court's claim of "consistent defer-
ence to Congress." Instead, he said a "more accurate description is
that the Court has tended to evade the hard issues when they arise
in the area of copyright law" (p. 4100). Furthermore, the Court
should not continue this tradition, especially as the legislative history of the 1976 Act shows that "Congress meant to change the old
pattern and enact a statute that would cover new technologies, as
well as old" (p. 4100). He portrayed the Court's approach as dra-
matically altering fair use and contributory infringement: "Should
Congress choose to respond to the Court's decision, the old doctrines can be resurrected. As it stands, however, the decision today erodes much of the coherence that these doctrines have
struggled to achieve" (p. 4110). Blackmun also identified two
kinds of Betamax uses as being at issue: time-shifting; and library
building.

Blackmun carefully analyzed Section 106, which grants copyright owners a variety of exclusive rights, and its explication in
the legislative history. He noted that the 1976 Act and its history
do specify some situations in which making a single copy is not an
infringement, for example, Section 108(a) permitting limited library copying and making a single copy for a blind person. If the
1976 Act had created a general exemption for making single copies, then it would have been unnecessary to discuss specific situations. "But neither the statute nor its legislative history suggests
any intent to create a general exemption for a single copy made for
personal or private use. Indeed, it appears that Congress considered and rejected the very possibility of a special private use exemption" (p. 4102). And, later in the opinion, he stated: "I therefore
find in the 1976 Act no implied exemption to cover the home taping of television programs, whether it be for a single copy, for private use, or for home use. Taping a copyrighted television program
is infringement unless it is permitted by the fair use exemption in
§107 of the 1976 Act" (p. 4105).

In discussing fair use, Blackmun noted the Supreme Court's
lack of guidance on what is fair use despite having dealt with it in
both *Williams & Wilkins* and *Benny* v. *Loew's*. (Both were decided
by equally divided courts; in the *Williams & Wilkins* case because
Blackmun himself took no part in the decision.) He also pointed
out that Congress failed to "provide definitive rules when it codified the fair use doctrine in the 1976 Act; it simply incorporated a
list of factors 'to be considered.' . . ." (p. 4105). These factors were
given no weights and not meant to be exclusive.

Fair use, according to Blackmun, permits a limited use of a

copyrighted work by a second author for the public good (see discussion of respondents' brief earlier in this section). He called it a "subsidy" at the first author's expense. His basic theme centered on *productive* uses for the public benefit as opposed to reproducing an entire work for an individual's sole benefit.

In summing up his remarks on fair use, Blackmun criticized the Supreme Court for ignoring two of the four criteria: the nature of the copyrighted work and the amount used. Since Betamax owners usually record entertainment shows, time-shifting is an infringement under the nature of work criteria. In terms of the amount used, the entire work is copied. Here, too, time-shifting fails to qualify as fair use: "Fair use is intended to allow individuals engaged in productive uses to copy small portions of original works that will facilitate their own productive endeavors" (p. 4111).

Blackmun opined that Sony's argument that time-shifting increases public access to material broadcast free over the public airwaves is a misconception of the nature of copyright. He compared the situation to borrowing a book from the public library. Just because you borrowed the book without charge does not mean you are free to copy the book any more than you are free to copy a purchased book. While it is tempting to stretch fair use to allow increased access to TV programming, Blackmun considered this an erosion of basic copyright protection: "Even in the context of highly productive educational uses, Congress has avoided this temptation; in passing the 1976 Act, Congress made it clear that off-the-air videotaping was to be permitted only in very limited situations" (p. 4107).

Blackmun also criticized the Court and district court for putting the burden of proof regarding economic harm on Universal and Disney. He supported the view that "a copyright owner need prove only a *potential* for harm to the market for or the value of the copyrighted work" (p. 4107). In this case, Universal and Disney had identified possible reductions in the rerun audiences, movie theater markets, and rental sales of prerecorded videotapes and discs. So, Blackmun found that time-shifting had a substantial adverse economic effect and, thus, could not be deemed fair use.

Moving on to the question of contributory infringement, Blackmun noted that liability for copyright infringement can include those who did not actually carry out the infringing activity. No direct contact is needed between the contributory infringer and the infringer. Thus, if off-the-air taping is a copyright infringement, "Sony has induced and materially contributed to the infringing conduct of Betamax owners" (p. 4109). The question is the amount of VTR usage that is infringing since, if a significant amount is not infringing, then there is no contributory infringement. However, the Supreme Court never addressed the amount of noninfringing use needed to absolve a manufacturer from contributory infringement. Therefore, Blackmun suggested remanding this issue to the district court for further consideration.

Blackmun then identified two serious flaws in the Supreme Court's finding that time-shifting is a fair use. First, the Court's reasoning centered on the claim that many copyright owners have no objection to time-shifting and Universal and Disney cannot prevent these owners from authorizing such recording of their programs. Second, the Court concluded that Sony was not liable for contributory infringement because even unauthorized time-shifting is fair use. To Blackmun, this conclusion was even more troubling: "There is no indication that the fair use doctrine has any application for purely personal consumption on the scale involved in this case, and the Court's application of it here deprives fair use of the major cohesive force that has guided evolution of the doctrine in the past" (p. 4111). And, he reiterated: "Purely consumptive uses are certainly not what the fair use doctrine was designed to protect, and the awkwardness of applying the statutory language to time-shifting only makes clearer that fair use was designed to protect only uses that are productive" (p. 4111). He therefore concurred with the Ninth Circuit that an award of damages or continuing royalties might be an "appropriate means of balancing the equities in this case" (p. 4112).

Several of the footnotes and asides in both the majority and dissenting opinions provided useful information and insights. For example, time-shifting was defined as "the practice of recording a program to view it once at a later time, and thereafter erasing it" (p. 4091). *My Man Godfrey* was identified as an uncopyrighted movie (p. 4096; but no mention was made of the status of the underlying rights). A request for an injunction banning VTRs was described as harmful to the prerecorded videotape market because no one buys software without access to the hardware.

Perhaps the most noteworthy of these comments was Blackmun's footnote concerning *Williams & Wilkins* (see earlier discussion). He said the Court's reasoning in this case was flawed. One, it is not clear that "hand copying" an entire work is permissible. There simply is no reported case, possibly because no copyright owner thought it worthwhile to sue. Two, hand copying and even typing are self-limiting. The drudgery of hand copying means "only necessary and fairly small portions of a work are taken" (p. 4103). Thus, harm is minimal. But modern copying technology has changed this.

Although home and educational off-air taping issues appear — at least in judicial thinking — to be separate entities, many educational and library organizations were concerned that any restrictions placed on home off-air taping would have an adverse effect on educational and library uses. Since the *Sony* decision did not cover educational uses — nor did it address "the transfer of tapes to other persons, the use of home-recorded tapes for public performances, or the copying of programs transmitted on pay or cable television systems" (pp. 4091–4092) — their concern now focuses on Congress. There is already a growing lobby for some type of value-added tax on blank tapes and recording equipment, both audio and video. But will Congress act? Representative Robert W. Kastenmeier (D-Wis.), chair of the House subcommittee that deals with copyright, said he doubted Congress would subject home taping to provisions of the copyright law. And what of educational off-air taping? *Sony* has changed nothing. *Plus ça change, plus c'est la même chose.*

Three CATV Cases. While CATV fell outside the scope of this study, *Fortnightly* v. *United Artists* (1969), *Walt Disney* v. *Alaska Television Network* (1969), and *Teleprompter* v. *CBS* (1974) give some indication of the judicial view of broadcasting. In *Fortnightly,* the question was whether or not the Fortnightly Corporation, owner and operator of CATV systems, *performed* United Artists' shows. The court observed that

> both broadcaster and viewer play crucial roles in the total television process. . . . One . . . as active performer; the other, as passive beneficiary.
>
> When CATV is considered in this framework, we conclude that it falls on the viewer's side of the line. Essentially, a CATV system no more than enhances the viewer's capacity to receive the broadcaster's signals. (p. 5)

The Supreme Court reversed the pro–United Artists decisions of the lower courts.

The difference between *Fortnightly* and *Walt Disney* v. *Alaska Television,* according to District Judge Goodwin, was the time or storage element. In *Fortnightly,* the time between the TV broadcast and its reception in the viewer's home was minimal. In this case, there was an average difference of one week during which the program was stored on videotape. Goodwin drew an analogy from audio: "Defendants could hardly contend that it would not be an infringement of copyright for one to receive the broadcast of a copyrighted song by way of radio, record it on a master disc, and then play it over another radio station or 'Musak' system" (p. 213). Looking at the possibility of economic harm, the Court commented:

> While the defendants did not make the video tapes available on a widespread basis, the tapes were *capable* of being sold to any cable television system with the proper equipment. Such a distribution could, and no doubt would, be in direct competition with the owner of the copyrighted materials contained . . . therein. (p. 213)

The court found for Disney.

Discussing its *Fortnightly* decision, the Supreme Court in *Teleprompter* (1974) distinguished a performance from a nonperformance activity. Broadcasters "performed," that is, they selected programs to be viewed and procured and propagated programs to the public. CATV "received and carried," but did not perform. It did not broadcast but simply carried what was there without editing. It also simply received programs released to the public and carried them to additional viewers. The court found for Teleprompter.

However, referring to *Fortnightly* and *Teleprompter* in his dissenting opinion to the *Sony* (1984) decision, Justice Blackmun noted that the two cases had been decided under the 1909 Act. Thus, the Supreme Court had held that the reception of a radio or TV broadcast was not a performance. This, according to Blackmun, has been overturned by the 1976 Act's broad definition of "perform": "To 'perform' a work means to recite, render, play, dance, or act it, either directly or by means of any device or process or, in the case of a motion picture or other audiovisual work, to show its images in any sequence or to make the sounds accompanying it audible" (Section 101).

SUMMARY

In the United States, copyright is an enumerated power whose chief purpose is to advance the public welfare by promoting artistic and scientific progress. The mechanism for encouraging such progress is economic reward. However, a conflict has arisen between the purpose, that is, public access to these works, and the mechanism, remuneration to the creator. Reconciliation attempts based on time limitation, ambit of protection, and two constitutional amendments have been proposed but found lacking. An underlying question of this conflict centers on the appropriateness of economic incentive as the mechanism for achieving the goal of copyright. A related issue focuses on the possibility that copyright, in its current form, has become obsolete. The answer to the first of these two soul-searching questions is a shaky affirmation of the role of economic reward in the copyright scheme. The answer to the second is unclear.

The judicially originated doctrine of fair use is the most favored resolution of the public-access-versus-economic-incentive issue, especially apropos of educational uses. However, never easy to define in the first place, its inclusion in Section 107 of the 1976 Copyright Act did not aid in its explication. Indeed, no precise definition is given of the doctrine; the criteria listed are exemplary; no indication of the ordering and weighting of such criteria is included; and fair and exempted use distinctions are blurred. In addition, the congressional discussions center on photocopying. Whether this preoccupation with photocopying resulted in the failure to define fair use for educational off-air taping is not clear. It may have been due to a reluctance on the part of Congress to delay further passing a revision act or, perhaps, a congressional reluctance to deal with such a controversial topic.

This lack of definition and delineation of fair use by Section 107 shifted the focus back to the courts, the originators of the fair use doctrine. However, there are few litigated cases addressing the issue of fair use and educational usage of copyrighted materials. Thus, case law must be analyzed to determine how the courts have generally defined the four fair use criteria identified in Section 107.

The first criterion is the purpose and character of the use. The courts note a distinction between commercial versus nonprofit educational purposes, rather than commercial versus noncommercial purposes. In addition, the courts distinguish between uses of a work designed to advance knowledge, for example, criticism and research, as opposed to mere commercial exploitation, such as an unauthorized quotation in an advertisement. However, the application of this criterion is greatly influenced by the third and fourth fair use factors.

Both case law and legislative history seem to ignore the second criterion, the nature of the copyrighted work, which is characterized as dealing with works informational in nature rather than those creatively inclined. In other words, a scientific, legal, medical, historical, or biographical work would have some scope for the use of prior copyrighted materials on the same subject. A show categorized as entertainment would be less likely to qualify for fair use.

Two approaches were identified in the analysis of the third criterion, the amount of a copyrighted work used. One approach is quantitative, based on the idea of a "substantial taking." This approach supports the contention that excessive copying of a copyrighted work is never fair use. The second approach was qualitative in nature, holding that an infringement could occur if the part copied is a crucial section of a work, regardless of the amount copied.

The fourth criterion, the economic effect, is considered the key factor by the courts and commentators alike. If the value of the original work is diminished, the copyright owner has been injured. In addition, the question of whether the subsequent work competes in the marketplace, at present or in the future, with the original work must be considered. Related to this is the question of whether the copy serves the same function as the original, in which case fair use is probably not available as a defense.

Copyright proprietors have litigated against individual teachers only twice. In both cases the teachers lost; claiming educational usage was in itself not a viable defense. The *BOCES* (1978, 1982, 1983) case involved large-scale, systematic off-air videotaping activities by an educational consortium. After a nonjury trial, the court granted the plaintiffs' motion for a permanent injunction against further unauthorized off-air taping activities. In its 1983 decision, the court also prohibited temporary off-air taping by BOCES. The availability of a variety of licensing arrangements with the plaintiffs seems to have been a key consideration in analyzing "harmful effect" and dismissing fair use as a defense. The court also noted that convenience, taken alone, was not an adequate basis for fair use.

Although home and educational off-air taping appear to be separate issues with little common ground, the *Sony* (1979, 1981, 1984) decisions warrant consideration. In light of its possible influence on the *BOCES* decisions, the Ninth Circuit's discussion of the 1976 Act and fair use is important. The court noted that the Act does not include convenience, entertainment, or increased access as purposes of fair use. In addition, fair use generally precludes a copy serving the same function as the original. Finally, the court supported the contention that off-air videotaping tends to diminish the potential market and therefore has an adverse economic effect. This decision was appealed to the U.S. Supreme Court, which reversed it. The Supreme Court's five to four decision in favor of Sony illustrated the prevalent polarization regarding fair use and time-shifting. Contrary to popular opinion, the Supreme Court actually addressed the issue of whether Sony was a contributory infringer. To answer this question, it first had to determine whether home off-air taping was an infringement. Whether Congress will now consider the issue is doubtful.

In *Fortnightly* (1968) and *Teleprompter* (1974), the U.S. Supreme Court discussed its definition of broadcasting. In both cases, the court decided that the CATV operation received and carried a signal but did not broadcast it. However, in *Walt Disney* v. *Alaska Television* (1969), the CATV operation stored the program on videotape for an average of a week. This interruption of the signal between the original telecast and the CATV showing was viewed as potentially harmful economically. Disney therefore won its case.

4

SUGGESTED SOLUTIONS

As noted earlier, Congress indicated that fair use had "some limited application" (H.R. 94-1476, p. 71) to the area of educational off-air videotape recording and recommended further exploration of the problem by concerned parties to find "a nonlegislative solution as to what constitutes fair use for broadcast audiovisual works" (*Hearings,* 1979, p. 3). Recommended solutions basically fall into one of two broad categories: licensing, and guidelines.

Among the alternatives to licensing and guidelines are the public service concept, that is, a special tax write-off for copyright owners, and the idea of taxing blank tapes in order to recompense copyright owners. Another notion is that producers should charge the networks more if the number of viewers and number of videotape recorders could be determined. This way, the consumer pays via the purchase of advertised products, since advertisers pay the networks who pay the producers.

LICENSING

According to Ringer (1976), compulsory licensing schemes evolve from a seven-stage process:

1. A copyright law is written at a particular point in the development of communications technology without thought for the future.
2. Further technological developments create new areas for creation and use of copyrighted works.

3. Business and industrial investments develop.
4. Since the law is ambiguous on rights and liabilities, no royalties are paid.
5. The courts reach the point where they can no longer resolve the issues; only Congress can solve the problem through new legislation.
6. Congress is faced with the lobbying efforts of special interest groups.
7. Congress needs a compromise and therefore turns to compulsory licensing.

Compulsory licensing was suggested as a means of mitigating possible economic harm resulting from off-air taping and of dealing with fair use and new media as early as 1964 (Fritch) – almost ten years before the first educational videotaping suit, *CBS* v. *Vanderbilt*, was filed. Krasilovsky (1969), another early supporter of this concept, wrote: "If low cost copyright licensing can be achieved, schools need not become dispensaries of prepackaged information and can achieve . . . [the] goal of being centers of intellectual and scholarly inquiry assisted by a positive use of technology" (p. 426). Crossland (1968) and Meyer (1971) were two other early advocates of such a system.

In his lower court *Williams & Wilkins* (1972) ruling, Commissioner Davis, commenting on the plaintiff's desire for a licensing program, observed that it seemed a logical and common-sense solution to the problem. A continuing royalty schedule was also favorably viewed by the Ninth Circuit in its *Sony* (1981) reversal. Furthermore, Curtin's order in the *BOCES* (1978) case stated: "Notwithstanding any provision in this order, the defendant BOCES is authorized to enter into licensing agreements with the plaintiffs for the use of their films" (cited in *Hearings*, 1979, p. 158). And, in Curtin's later *BOCES* decisions (1982, 1983), the availability of a variety of licensing arrangements played an important role in the finding of economic harm to the plaintiffs and therefore the inapplicability of fair use.

Seltzer (1977) noted that statutory controls for access and price – for example, compulsory licensing – have reaffirmed copyright's essential reliance on monetary incentives. Lee and Laterza (1977) urged compulsory licenses as a means for allowing educational institutions to use copyrighted materials. And many media producers have indicated a willingness to participate in a clearance process that would do away with fair use. The question is whether the educational community would willingly participate in such a system. Advantages of a compulsory license to educators include freedom from the ambiguities of fair use and its interpretation and unrestricted use of copyrighted materials.

Further support for a compulsory licensing scheme comes from the Act itself for its single, most dominant trend was the use of compulsory licenses as a means of balancing public access and economic reward to creators. Section 111(d) outlined the compulsory licensing for cable television's secondary transmissions; Section 115 for making and distributing phonorecords of nondramatic musical works; Section 116(b) for the public performance of works by means of a coin-operated phonorecord player; and Section 118 for "use of certain works in connection with noncommercial broadcasting." The resulting royalties from Sections 111, 116, and 118 are to be handled by the Copyright Royalty Tribunal created and described in Sections 801-810 of the Act.

Tseng (1979) reviewed 12 proposed solutions to the photoduplication problem. Among them was a compulsory licensing system for nonprofit institutional photocopying resembling Section 115 of the 1976 Act. Others were based on individually negotiated licenses and the establishment of a publishers' consortium. A cross between these last two seems to have been established under Films Incorporated, the largest nontheatrical U.S. distributor "of quality films, videotapes, and other AV material for education and entertainment" ("A Few Words About the TLC," 1980, p. 2).

Called the Television Licensing Center (TLC),* its executive director is Ivan Bender, formerly of the Copyright Office and a strong advocate of licensing. The TLC described itself as follows:

> A national single-source clearinghouse established to provide educators with information about off-air videotaping and with licenses to record, duplicate and retain television programming. It offers educators a convenient and legal mechanism for capturing the best of television at a fraction of the usual AV costs. It ensures producers the copyright protection to which they are entitled. ("A Few Words About the TLC," p. 2)

However, the TLC was not created by congressional legislation – nor has it received official acknowledgment. It was established by a number of producers to fill the void created by a lack of guidelines on educational off-air taping and the continued unsuccessful negotiations to bridge the gap. But since it does not represent all producers and all programs, even this unofficial attempted solu-

*This is not an endorsement of the TLC.

tion leaves educational institutions with no one-stop licensing center.

To become a member, an institution signs a TLC master license, which allows it to tape legally any TLC program for a 45-day evaluation (compare the discussion of guidelines that follows). At the end of that period, the institution either keeps the tape by licensing it or erases it ("How to Become a TLC Member," 1981).

A sample of its October 1980 licensing fees included the following:

1. One copy of "The Royal Archives of Ebla," a 60-minute program, could be licensed for a $50 annual fee or a $125 life-of-the-tape fee ("Taping and Duplication Fees," 1980, p. 3).
2. The 13 "Cosmos" programs could be taped, duplicated, and shown over closed-circuit delivery in one building at an annual fee of $325 per set for one to three complete sets of the series, $812.50 per set for a five-year license, $162.50 per set annually for six or more sets, or $406.25 per set for six or more sets for a five-year license. For small schools, that is, those with enrollments under 600, a special fee of $130 for one year or $325 for five years was quoted. Individual shows within the series ran from $25 for one year or $62.50 for five years for one copy to $12.50 per copy for one year or $31.25 for five years for six or more copies ("Taping and Duplication Fees," p. 5; compare Troost, 1981, discussed in Chapter 2).
3. "The Body in Question," consisting of 13 programs, began its schedule at one complete set for $650 for one year or $1625 for the life of the tape. Individual programs were $50 for one year or $125 for the life of the tape for a single copy; a master and duplicate (two tapes), $75 for one year or $187.50 for the life of the tape ("Taping and Duplication Fees," p. 6).

Probably the best-known example of a clearinghouse system is that of the American Society of Composers, Authors and Publishers, usually referred to by its acronym, ASCAP. ASCAP was established in the early part of the century, when two things became apparent: (1) composers and publishers could no longer count on sheet music sales for most of their income but would need to look to performances of their works; and (2) musical performers, for the most part, had no time or reasonable means of negotiating separate licenses for each work performed (Finkelstein, 1966). These two concerns are echoed in today's debates over photocopying and off-air taping.

To solve the music industry's problem, ASCAP developed a clearinghouse to accommodate (1) users needing ready access to many works and (2) copyright owners whose works might be simultaneously used by many users. The system is based almost entirely on blanket licenses whose fees are developed by means of a weighted formula that takes into consideration such factors as the type of performance, for example, a symphony versus a commercial jingle. Changes in the formula must be approved by the federal court overseeing ASCAP and the entire ASCAP membership. Some licensees, such as TV networks and Muzak-type firms, must send documentation. Local radio and TV are randomly sampled by an independent agency. The documentation and sampling results are processed and converted into quarterly payments. After expenses are deducted, half the amount goes to the writers as a group; the other half, to the publishers as a group. These two groups then distribute the fees to their members based on the performance surveys. In addition to handling its own members, ASCAP also clears foreign composers and publishers (Finkelstein, 1966).

The issue of licensing has not been without its opponents and critics. Ringer (1976) characterized compulsory licensing as a loss of control. Authors lose the right to control their own work; they cannot grant anyone an exclusive license for a specified purpose. Their work is lumped with thousands of others. The author becomes a unit in a large collective system with blanket royalties; the individuality of author and work alike tends to be lost. The increased reliance on compulsory licensing is changing copyright from a creator's exclusive right to a scheme for ensuring a copyright proprietor some remuneration for−but no control over−a work's use. She also worried about the evolution of the Copyright Royalty Tribunal. In many ways, it is

> a sensible and ingenious device for making the various compulsory licensing schemes work efficiently and without constant and unwarranted litigation and need for congressional action. At the same time, the existence of a government body that is paying out royalties, settling disputes among copyright owners, reviewing royalty rates, and deciding the terms and rates of licenses, seems an open invitation to further government control. (Ringer, 1977b, p. 203)

Gold (*Hearings*, 1979), representing three Public Broadcasting Service (PBS) affiliates, opposed compulsory licensing on two grounds. First, such a license may cause problems with the guilds as their fees may be greater than what the license brings in. Second, individuals and organizations who currently derive their primary revenues from the educational community may perceive a serious economic threat in compulsory licensing. If so, those that in the past have televised their materials may refuse to do so in the future. The result will be a loss of valuable programming for the viewer.

Educators opposed licensing schemes because they support the concept of fair use, which does not require a royalty payment.

Callison (1981) noted two problems faced by educators trying to establish a fair and equitable licensing fee structure. The first centers on the lack of time to gain copying permission. In other words, as teachers are often unaware of a program's telecast until the day or week before, sending a letter requesting off-air taping permission is useless. Also, class discussions often spark a spontaneous need for additional materials. The second problem is that, even given advance notice, it is difficult to locate the correct person to contact for permission. I encountered both problems in conducting a survey of producers' stands on the off-air taping guidelines, the results of which are presented in Appendix E. Answers to the survey questionnaire mailed in December were still arriving well into March. In a classroom situation, such a delay in receiving an answer would make the original taping request useless since the class would have continued on to the next unit and the optimum teaching moment would have been lost. Also, I found that the Association of Media Producers' *Directory of Rights & Permission Officers* (circa 1978), for example, is out of date, and *E&ITV's* annual directory of video program sources does not cover all organizations.

However, these types of problems would not arise under a compulsory licensing scheme. The off-air taping guidelines discussed next are another attempt at solving these types of problems.

OFF-AIR TAPING GUIDELINES
FOR EDUCATIONAL PURPOSES

The push for guidelines to delineate what is or is not fair use came from educators. Congressional intent also supported this approach. As the guidelines agreed upon for classroom photocopying and educational uses of music were incorporated into legislative history, so too were guidelines for off-air educational taping to be included. The problem was that the concerned parties had trouble defining the minimum levels of off-air copying in terms similar to those included in the guidelines for print materials and musical compositions.

To help resolve this impasse, the Copyright Office and Ford Foundation sponsored the Conference on Video Recording for Educational Uses at Airlie House, Virginia, on July 19–22, 1977. Although the Airlie House Conference, as it came to be called brought together a wide range of concerned parties, nothing substantive in terms of negotiations resulted. The months passed, negotiations broke down, and as Representative Kastenmeier noted in the 1979 hearings,

> producers . . . [began] to institute lawsuits against educators and in some cases . . . attempted to withhold product from the broadcast market. These developments are not consistent with congressional intent to write a law which will assure widespread dissemination of intellectual creations while assuring a fair reward for the authors of those creations.

Thus, the congressional subcommittee dealing with copyright—the Subcommittee on Courts, Civil Liberties, and the Administration of Justice, chaired by Representative Robert W. Kastenmeier (D-Wis.)—convened a hearing on March 2, 1979, to encourage the concerned parties to work out an agreement so that Congress would not have to institute a full-scale reexamination of the issue.

At the hearing on educational off-air taping, various issues and suggestions for guidelines were aired (*Hearings*, 1979, for example, pp. 55; 57; 78; 94; 166; 173; 178–180). An ad hoc committee composed of representatives from the concerned parties was then appointed to negotiate the guidelines based on the testimony presented. The committee deliberated two years before reaching a consensus on fair use provisions. On October 14, 1981, Representative Kastenmeier inserted the off-air guidelines into the *Congressional Record*. In addition to the guidelines, he included the negotiating committee's August 31, 1981, guidelines' transmittal letter, as well as reaction letters from the Motion Picture Association of America (MPAA) and the Association of Media Producers (AMP).

According to the committee's announcement, the guidelines specify all the important parameters, including retention periods and use in classrooms, similar places devoted to instruction, and for home-bound instruction. The text of the guidelines is quite simple and straightforward (see Appendix D).

Potential Problems

A closer look at the guidelines, however, reveals certain weaknesses. First, when Kastenmeier's subcommittee accepted the guidelines and inserted them into the *Congressional Record,* they became part of the copyright law's legislative history, as had the print and music guidelines earlier. While these guidelines will probably be considered by the courts when making a ruling, legislative history (as previously discussed) does not have the force of law, nor are the courts bound by it. In other words, the assumption is that the courts will turn to the guidelines when faced with fair use decisions. But whether the courts will actually adopt the guidelines, and to what extent, is unknown.*

Discussing the legal impact of guidelines from a different perspective, Nimmer (1981) observed:

> It would appear that the courts are not bound by the guidelines . . . in view of the stated legislative intent that "Section 107 is intended to restate the present [pre-1978] judicial doctrine of fair use . . ." [H.R. 94-1476, p. 66]. Strictly speaking, the guidelines represent merely the Congressional Committees' "understanding" of what the courts would regard as fair use. . . . Congress does not purport to substitute its judgment for that of the courts in any particular case. Nevertheless, it seems clear that the courts will be greatly influenced by this "understanding," so that for practical purposes the guidelines may usually be regarded as the equivalent of statutory text. (section 13.05[E].)

Nimmer's view of the guidelines' legal impact appears to be supported by the negotiating committee. According to Eileen Cooke (1981), one of the negotiating committee's co-chairs, the negotiating committee could not bind the courts to a particular interpretation of the law. However, the joint issuance of the guidelines reflects how fair use could be satisfactorily implemented for the mutual interest of proprietors, educators, and students.

Jacqueline Weiss (1982), associate general counsel for PBS, asked Representative Kastenmeier's staff counsel what weight the guidelines would carry. The staff counsel replied

> that they are prepared to stand behind the Guidelines and do everything possible to make clear that it is Congress' intent that the

*The guidelines for classroom photocopying of print materials played a role in the out-of-court settlement between publishers and New York University. However, Judge Curtin denied BOCES the right to tape off-the-air for temporary use (see Chapter 3).

Guidelines represent the appropriate policy behind the fair use doctrine with respect to off-air taping for educational purposes. Furthermore, he indicated that "if educators are sued, and they end up
losing, Congress is undoubtedly going to consider that the courts
haven't properly construed the law, and they'll change it." (p. 2)

Another problem with the guidelines is that they are, in a nar-
row sense, merely a gentlemen's agreement between the organizations agreeing to honor them. And it may not be safe to apply the
guidelines indiscriminately to all producers (see Appendix E).

The lower *Williams & Wilkins* (1972) court, in reference to the
1935 "Gentlemen's Agreement," remarked: "The 'gentlemen's
agreement' does not have, nor has it ever had, the force of law with
respect to what constitutes copyright infringement or 'fair use' "
(p. 680). Tseng (1979), discussing the guidelines for printed material, noted that the terms of the fair use guidelines may be binding
only upon those who subscribe to them. In that instance, both the
American Association of University Professors (AAUP) and the
Association of American Law Schools had disassociated themselves from the guidelines, claiming they were too restrictive for
their teaching purposes. Professor John Stedman (1977), chair of
AAUP's Committee on Copyright Law Revision, pointed out that,
regardless of the guidelines' effect on the signatories and their incorporation into the legislative history, they were not binding
upon persons or groups not party to the arrangements. He maintained that guidelines are not binding rules but useful devices for
keeping within appropriate bounds.

Reminiscent of this disassociation by two educational organizations from the photocopying guidelines is the reaction of the
MPAA and the AMP to the off-air taping guidelines as inserted
into the *Congressional Record* together with the guidelines. On
August 23, 1981, James Bouras of the MPAA wrote to Leonard
Wasser of the Writers Guild of America, East, to notify him that,
even though the MPAA was party to the guideline formulation
discussions, the MPAA, as such, would take no position on the
new guidelines. However, Bouras did indicate that seven individ-
ual member companies of the MPAA assented to the guidelines:
Avco Embassy Pictures, Columbia Pictures, Filmways Pictures,
Metro-Goldwyn-Mayer, Paramount Pictures, Twentieth Century
Fox, and Universal Pictures.

Even more disquieting is the September 17, 1981, letter from
Gordon Nelson, president of the AMP, to Representative Kastenmeier. Despite the AMP's participation on the negotiating committee, the AMP's board of directors voted not to endorse the

guidelines because they feared the guidelines would "jeopardize the future well-being of the small but vital educational media industry, its market, and the availability of a broad variety of instructional materials essential to maintaining quality education programs" (p. E4752).

According to Scully (1981), Sheldon E. Steinbach, a member of the negotiating committee and general counsel for the American Council on Education, remarked that "while the committee expects educational institutions to follow the guidelines, several lawsuits over the issue probably would be required 'to put some meat on them' " (p. 11). This seems a direct contradiction of the purpose of the guidelines, that is, the establishment of clear standards for both copyright proprietors and users.

Yet another problem with the guidelines, one that may contribute to the lawsuits predicted by Steinbach, is the question of who enforces adherence to them. The guidelines currently leave enforcement in control of each individual educational institution (see Appendix D, point 9). There is no independent organization to oversee their implementation. This could lead to abuses (for example, retaining the tapes beyond the time permitted), which would damage the integrity of the guidelines. As noted in Chapter 1, the publishing industry already instigated litigation in order to help enforce the classroom photocopying guidelines.

Cooke (1981) observed that educators may sometimes find situations where strict adherence to the guidelines interferes with legitimate educational procedures. In such cases, educators may deem "uses beyond the guidelines to be appropriate, fair, and within the law" (p. 664). Conversely, she also pointed out that the guidelines do not constrain copyright owners from claiming an infringement when they find what they consider to be an unfair application of the agreed-upon guidelines.

A final weakness of the guidelines is the threat of rigidity. Pitt (1977) warned that a strict construction of the guidelines by either the courts, educators, or copyright owners could freeze educational fair use within the parameters of the current guidelines, thus seriously impairing its viability as a judicial doctrine. The negotiating committee appears to have had similar forebodings, for in its August 31, 1981, letter to Representative Kastenmeier it suggested that the guidelines be periodically reviewed.

Applying the Guidelines

The negotiating committee stressed that the guidelines are limited to nonprofit educational institutions. In other words, profit-making schools and organizations that are not part of a formal educational process are excluded from the guideline mechanism. The committee also stressed that the TV programs involved are those telecast for reception by the public without charge. This includes programs that are being simultaneously retransmitted by a cable system but excludes, for example, pay cable, pay television, and Instructional Television Fixed Service.

Representative Kastenmeier noted in his October 14, 1981, remarks that specific permissions from copyright proprietors may still be required for uses not covered in the guidelines. When asked if, given the new guidelines, licensing was still necessary, Eleanor English (1982), associate director of educational services at KCET, the Los Angeles PBS station, answered with an emphatic "Yes!" Similarly, the negotiating committee, in its August 31, 1981, letter, observed that specific licenses and permissions may still be required. In addition, the committee explained that the guidelines are not meant to allow teachers – under the guise of fair use – to substitute intentionally off-air taping "for a standard practice of purchase or license of the same educational material by the institution concerned" (p. E4751). Thus, the off-air taping guidelines do not automatically preclude the need for a license or letter of permission to tape a television broadcast.

To license a PBS broadcast, Ms. English (1982) suggested that a written request include the name of the series; the type of use, for instance, whether the program will be used strictly in the library or will be the basis of a course; and whether the program will be used in a single classroom or transmitted over a closed-circuit network. In terms of PBS programs, if a series is used as a course for credit, then the number of times the program is to be shown must be included in the licensing request. A license for a televised course of instruction offered for credit averages $300 per course and $15 per student.

According to Ms. Weiss (1982) of PBS, key points to remember in applying the guidelines include the following:

1. Taping in anticipation of requests is not allowed.
2. Regardless of the number of times a show is broadcast, it may only be recorded once at the request of the *same* teacher.
3. In order to make multiple copies of a program, the requests from each individual teacher must have been received *prior* to the actual taping.
4. A recorded show may only be used *once* in the course of relevant teaching activities. However, if a teacher decides additional reinforcement is necessary, it may be shown once more.

5. A recorded show may not be used for noninstructional, entertainment purposes.
6. A recorded program may be transmitted over closed circuit as long as the transmission is to a single building, cluster, or campus.
7. A recorded program may only be shown to students within the first ten consecutive school days after the date of taping.
8. After the first ten consecutive school days, the tape may only be used by teachers for evaluation purposes only.
9. The copyright notice of the original broadcast must be included in the taped program.
10. A taped show need not be used in its entirety. For example, a 20-minute segment or two separate 10-minute segments may be excerpted for use as long as the original content is not altered.
11. Educational institutions must establish appropriate control procedures in order to maintain the integrity of the guidelines.

As noted in Chapter 2, PBS has had its own guidelines apropos of educational off-air taping. According to Eleanor English (1982), the new guidelines supersede the old PBS ones in most cases. The official PBS statement on this issue noted that, due to the greater benefits of the new guidelines, PBS will only issue details for programs where off-air copying rights exceeding the ten consecutive school days rule have been obtained. To do otherwise, the statement concluded, would only undermine the effectiveness of the new guidelines and cause confusion (Weiss, 1982).

ALTERNATIVES TO LICENSING AND GUIDELINES

Although licensing and guidelines are the two most recommended solutions, others have been suggested. Two that have received some attention are tax breaks and the taxing of blank tapes.

The idea of tax breaks or tax credit has been suggested by F. William Troost (see, for example 1977, 1983). Basically, his idea is that, in exchange for allowing unlimited educational use of their programs broadcast over the public airwaves, the producers or networks would be able to claim a tax credit. Since this tax credit would be in the public interest, it has also been called the public service concept.

The tax credit would be a set percentage (6–10 percent) of the total production costs or the amount paid by networks for the right to air the program. According to Troost, implementation of this recommendation would only affect tax laws and not require the creation of additional federal or private agencies. However, opponents claim that it is impractical and shows little understanding of the media industry. The basic problem with Troost's concept, they say, is that it trades off educational *uses* with *production costs*. It also fails to provide any compensation for "quantity uses." In other words, a good product is used many times, but the copyright owner will not receive any compensation for the many times the product is used.

The idea of placing some type of special tax on blank videotapes and distributing the amount collected as royalties has been gaining some support. In fact, currently under consideration by Congress are bills (such as S. 31, introduced in January 1983 to amend the 1976 Act with respect to home recording) that would impose a surcharge not only on blank videotapes but on audiotapes as well as on video- and audiorecording equipment. Some legislation would impose this only on the manufacturers or importers of the software and hardware. However, it seems reasonable to assume that the additional cost would be passed on to the purchaser. This cost has been estimated to range from $50 to $100 on equipment and $1 on tapes. Opponents claim this would place an unfair burden on those who use recorders and tapes for other than off-air taping.

SUMMARY

Licensing and guidelines comprise the major nonlegislative solutions for delineating fair use of broadcast copyrighted works.

Compulsory licensing is characterized as a compromise measure implemented by the legislature when the courts can no longer resolve the issues and the lobbying of special interest groups snarls the passage of new legislation. Such licensing has received strong support from the courts, commentators, and copyright proprietors alike. Further support comes from the reliance of the 1976 Copyright Act on compulsory licenses as a means of balancing the interests of the creators and users of copyrighted works in several other areas.

Critics have charged that compulsory licensing results in the copyright owner's loss of control over his own work. In addition, such licenses seem to invite greater government control. Moreover, the fees generated by the licenses may be smaller than the fees demanded by the various guilds involved in a TV production. Finally, licensing is perceived by some as a threat to the media industry.

An unofficial licensing clearinghouse for TV programs has been established under Films Incorporated. It is called the Television Licensing Center (TLC). After signing a master agreement, a member institution may tape any TLC program for a 45-day evaluation. At the end of the evaluation period, the tape can be kept if licensed; otherwise it must be erased. A better-known example of how a clearinghouse can serve both users and copyright owners is ASCAP, which is well established in the music world. It uses blanket licenses and fees based on weighted formulas. Such clearinghouses resolve the problem of locating the copyright owner for permission. They also provide a solution to the dilemma of having enough time to gain copying permission.

On October 14, 1981, the four-year search for off-air taping guidelines ended. Unlike the detailed guidelines by format that characterized those agreed upon for photocopying, the off-air taping one listed nine key points.

There are several areas for potential problems with the guidelines. The first is that, as legislative history, they lack the force of statutory law. The second is that not every copyright proprietor has agreed to the guidelines. The Association of Media Producers (AMP) and Training Media Distributors Association (TMDA) did not endorse the guidelines at all, whereas the Motion Picture Association of America (MPAA), with the exception of a few individual member companies, took no position at all. A corollary to this is that litigation may be necessary in order to refine the application of the guidelines and establish their worth. Finally, there is a chance that the guidelines may freeze the concept of educational fair use.

The new guidelines are limited to nonprofit educational institutions taping programs broadcast to the general public without charge. Efficient record keeping is essential for the proper application of the guidelines. Teachers' requests, dates of taping, times shown, and number of copies taped are the key data that must be tracked in order to comply with the guidelines. Most important of all, the guidelines do not preclude the need for licensing.

Some alternatives to licensing and guidelines have been suggested. The idea of a tax credit to producers in return for unlimited educational taping of TV broadcasts is one of these alternatives. Another is imposing some type of surcharge on recording media and/or equipment to generate royalty fees, which would then be distributed.

5

WHERE ARE WE?

COURT INTERPRETATIONS

Section 107 of the 1976 Copyright Act did not freeze the doctrine of fair use but merely restated the current judicial thinking, and therefore old case law, points of law, rulings, judgments, and opinions retain their validity. Thus, both old and new cases must be consulted when interpreting the copyright law.

The courts have devoted special attention to four key criteria for fair use of copyrighted material: purpose of the use; character of the use of the copyrighted work; amount used; and economic effect of such a use. Based on these criteria, the courts distinguished between commercial and nonprofit educational—as distinct from noncommercial—purposes and usages. Works designed to advance knowledge, such as criticisms or research studies of a scientific, legal, medical, historical, or biographical nature, were given more scope for the use of prior copyrighted materials on the same subject than works commercially exploitative in nature. Similarly, the courts granted informational works more scope than those creatively inclined.

The courts—with two exceptions—consistently denied a fair use defense in cases of extensive copying. The first exception was the U.S. Supreme Court's decision in *Williams & Wilkins* (1975), which said that library photocopying of an entire journal article was fair use. However, the decision was rendered by an equally divided court and thus was not binding upon other courts as to principles of law. Furthermore, Section 108 was included in the 1976 Copyright Act in order to resolve the problem posed by this case. The second exception was the U.S. Supreme Court's decision in *Sony* (1984), which said that home off-air-taping was not an infringement of copyright and, therefore, Sony was not liable for contributory infringement. The courts also found that, regardless of the amount copied, an infringement could occur if the segment copied was especially crucial to the original work.

Economic effect was regarded by the courts as a critical factor. If the copy diminishes the value of the original, or may do so in the future, the copyright owner has been injured. In addition, if the copy served the same function as the original, fair use was less likely to be accepted as a defense.

Only twice have copyright proprietors litigated against individual educators. In both cases, the teacher lost. A claim of standard educational practice and usage was in itself not accepted as a viable defense. Large-scale and systematic off-air taping activities, such as that by an educational consortium, has been found an infringement of copyright. In *Encyclopaedia Britannica Educational Corporation* v. *Crooks* (1978, 1982, 1983), the court granted the plaintiffs a permanent injunction against such unauthorized off-air taping activities and prohibited temporary off-air taping. The court pointed to the availability of various licensing agreements as a key factor in its decisions.

In addition, the judiciary indicated that federal funding of a private firm's film production does not automatically preclude that firm from copyrighting that film. The courts also asserted that First Amendment concerns do not support the increased copying of copyrighted materials as a means of access.

FAIR USE

With the passing of the 1976 Copyright Act, the doctrine of fair use received statutory recognition for the first time. It had originated in the courts when it became apparent that a literal construction of the copyright proprietor's exclusive rights could hinder the progress of the arts and sciences, contrary to the constitutional mandate of copyright. In other words, the quintessential justification of the fair use doctrine comes from the original constitutional purpose in granting copyright protection. The courts developed fair use as a means of resolving the conflict between the public access and economic incentive phrases of the constitutional mandate for copyright.

A second reason given by the courts to support fair use is *de minimus non curat lex* – the law does not concern itself with trifles. This reason is based on the assumption that an insignificant portion of a protected work can be copied. Extensive copying is not generally accepted by the courts.

PUBLIC ACCESS

As with fair use, the courts have supported the public access principle because of the basic purpose of copyright as enunciated in the Constitution: the advancement of the public welfare through the promotion of artistic and scientific endeavors. The courts interpreted this to mean that public access has priority over the creator's economic reward. However, achieving the correct balance between proper access and proper reward has not been easy. Thus, the courts developed the idea–expression dichotomy. The idea–expression dichotomy maintains that an idea is *not* copyrightable; only the expression used to convey it can be copyrighted. In this way, the public has access to new ideas that further the progress of the arts and sciences, while the rewards for a particular work go to the creator.

In addition to the original constitutional mandate on copyright, the First Amendment has been championed as a basis for public access to copyrighted works. The courts, however, have been hesitant to accept it as such. Instead, the courts have interpreted the First Amendment copyright argument in terms of the idea–expression dichotomy.

SUGGESTED SOLUTIONS

Licensing and guidelines are the two major solutions suggested for resolving the educational off-air taping dilemma. Compulsory licensing has been a dominant trend in the current Copyright Act for balancing public access and economic reward. A clearinghouse system would be established to collect and distribute fees. Such a system would resolve the problems of locating copyright owners for permission to tape and having enough time to ask for the permission. Education would thus be able to avail itself of materials of immediate classroom importance without the accompanying worries.

The recently negotiated off-air taping guidelines are another solution. The guidelines limit themselves to nonprofit educational institutions taping programs broadcast to the general public without charge. The nine points discussed in the guidelines provide important parameters for retention periods, multiple copying, and location of use. However, not every producer has endorsed these guidelines.

To implement the guidelines, an efficient record-keeping system is essential. Teachers' written requests for the taping of a show must be received *prior* to the taping date. The exact date of the taping must be noted and the end of its corresponding 45-day retention period identified. For each copy of a show taped, there must be a written teacher's request received prior to the event. Tabs must be kept on the number of times a teacher airs the tape in a class—twice is the maximum. Each time a teacher requests a taping, the request must be checked to assure that the same teacher has not previously requested the taping of that particular show. Most important of all, specific licenses and permissions may still be required.

A written request (on school letterhead stationery) for permission to tape or a license should include several pieces of information: the name of the program (in the case of a series, whether the request is for the entire series or an individual show will probably make a big difference in the granting or rejecting of the request); the date of the taping; the retention period required; the number of times the tape will be shown; whether the tape will be used strictly in the library or is intended for classroom instruction; and, finally, whether the tape is to be transmitted over a closed circuit or similar network.

SOME FINAL THOUGHTS

Copyright, especially as it pertains to educational uses, is an ever-evolving mechanism. Even now there may be a court suit pending that will change some aspect of the educational utilization of copyright. Thus, educators must continue to monitor both statutory and case law.

The guidelines do not distinguish between types of producers; for instance, motion picture producers are treated the same as small educational media producers. This lack of distinction may have been a factor in producers' decisions not to endorse the guidelines. Similarly, types of shows have not been differentiated. Daily game and talk shows, weekly sitcom and adventure series, prime-time movies, documentary debates, and entertainment specials are all as one under the guidelines. This, too, may have influenced the Association of Media Producers (AMP), the Motion Picture Association of America (MPAA), and the Training Media Distributors Association (TMDA), among others, in their decisions apropos of the guidelines.

While the recently negotiated educational off-air taping guidelines provide much-needed parameters, they may only apply to selected telecasts. The dissenting letters from the AMP and MPAA, which were inserted into the legislative history with the guidelines, raise a serious question: Can a television program copyrighted by one of the organizations that has not assented to the guidelines be taped off the air per the guidelines? For example, can an educational institution, acting within the new guidelines, tape a program copyrighted by National Geographic, Encyclopaedia Britannica Educational Corporation, or Walt Disney Productions? Currently, there is no clear answer. Thus, educational institutions should be wary when taping a program. If the copyright owner has not agreed to the guidelines, special permission may be necessary in order to tape off the air.

Due to this uncertainty about using the guidelines, several recommendations suggest themselves. The first is to implement the suggestion of the off-air taping guidelines committee calling for a periodic review of the guidelines. Congress saw fit to require a report on the implementation of Section 108 every five years. Why not a similar report on the implementation of the guidelines? A related recommendation centers on surveys – similar to those for Section 108 – of producers, educational off-air taping, and compliance with the guidelines. The information from these surveys would be used to review the guidelines. Another recommendation (which will probably meet with much criticism from some quarters) is to reexamine the possibility of compulsory licensing and an ASCAP-type clearinghouse system. While such an approach would resolve many of the current issues, it need not affect the traditional fair use areas of criticism, comment, and news reporting.

Appendix A

SECTION 108 (F)(3)
OF THE 1976 COPYRIGHT ACT

108. Limitations on exclusive rights: Reproduction by libraries and archives

(a) Notwithstanding the provisions of section 106, it is not an infringement of copyright for a library or archives, or any of its employees acting within the scope of their employment, to reproduce no more than one copy or phonorecord, under the conditions specified by this section, if —

(1)   the reproduction or distribution is made without any purpose of direct or indirect commercial advantage;

(2)   the collections of the library or archives are (i) open to the public, or (ii) available not only to researchers affiliated with the library or archives or with the institution of which it is a part, but also to other persons doing research in a specialized field; and

(3)   the reproduction or distribution of the work includes a notice of copyright.

(f) Nothing in this section —

(3)   shall be construed to limit the reproduction and distribution by lending of a limited number of copies and excepts by a library or archives of an audiovisual news program, subject to clauses (1), (2), and (3) of subsection (a); . . .

Appendix B
SECTION 107
OF THE 1976 COPYRIGHT ACT

107. Limitations on exclusive rights: Fair use

Notwithstanding the provisions of section 106, the fair use of a copyrighted work, including such use by reproduction in copies or phonorecords or by any other means specified by that section, for purposes such as criticism, comment, news reporting, teaching (including multiple copies for classroom use), scholarship, or research, is not an infringement of copyright. In determining whether the use made of a work in any particular case is a fair use the factors to be considered shall include—

    (1) the purpose and character of the use, including whether such use is of a commercial nature or is for nonprofit educational purposes;

    (2) the nature of the copyrighted work;

    (3) the amount and substantiality of the portion used in relation to the copyrighted work as a whole; and

    (4) the effect of the use upon the potential market for or value of the copyrighted work.

Appendix C
PUBLIC BROADCASTING SERVICE
TAPING GUIDELINES

JOINT STATEMENT OF POLICY

**School Rerecording of Public
and Instructional Television
Programs**

November 1975

With the increased capability for off-air rerecording of educationally useful television programs for replay at times convenient to
classroom scheduling, it is important to school systems that public and instructional programs be available for classroom play-
back, closed-circuit display and other school exhibition modes
contemporaneously with local station broadcast. Content copyright and other legal limitations, however, often demand that the
use of such program rerecordings be controlled in a manner consistent with original television broadcast authorization.

Accordingly, the below signatory agencies have jointly agreed
on the general policy of authorizing supplemental school rerecordings of public and instructional television programs distributed
by them for local ETV and other educational broadcast, solely on
condition that:

1. School rerecordings may be made only by students, teachers,
    and faculty or staff members in an accredited non-profit educa-
    tional institution;

117

2. School rerecordings will be used solely for classroom, auditorium, or laboratory exhibition in the course of classroom instruction or related educational activities;
3. School rerecordings will be used only in the educational institution for which made, and will not be given away, loaned or otherwise made available outside that educational institution;
4. School rerecordings will be used only during the seven-day period of local ETV and other educational broadcast licensed by the distribution agency, and will be erased or destroyed immediately at the end of that seven-day period except to the extent specifically authorized in writing in advance by the distribution agency.

The signatory agencies have agreed that this supplemental school rerecording authorization will be applicable to all public and instructional programs distributed by them, excluding only those prohibited by reason of production or distribution rights restrictions.

Public Broadcasting Service
Public Television Library
Great Plains National Instructional Television Library
Agency for Instructional Television

Appendix D
EDUCATIONAL OFF-AIR TAPING GUIDELINES

GUIDELINES FOR OFF-AIR RECORDING OF BROADCAST PROGRAMMING FOR EDUCATIONAL PURPOSES

In March of 1979, Congressman Robert Kastenmeier, Chairman of the House Subcommittee on Courts, Civil Liberties and Administration of Justice, appointed a Negotiating Committee consisting of representatives of education organizations, copyright proprietors, and creative guilds and unions. The following guidelines reflect the Negotiating Committee's consensus as to the application of "fair use" to the recording, retention and use of television broadcast programs for educational purposes. They specify periods of retention and use of such off-air recordings in classrooms and similar places devoted to instruction and for home-bound instruction. The purpose of establishing these guidelines is to provide standards for both owners and users of copyrighted television programs.

1. The guidelines were developed to apply only to off-air recording by non-profit educational institutions.
2. A broadcast program may be recorded off-air simultaneously with broadcast transmission (including simultaneous cable retransmission) and retained by a non-profit educational institution for a period not to exceed the first forty-five (45) consecutive calendar days after date of recording. Upon conclusion of such retention period, all off-air recordings must be erased or destroyed immediately. "Broadcast programs" are television

programs transmitted by television stations for reception by the general public without charge.

3. Off-air recordings may be used once by individual teachers in the course of relevant teaching activities, and repeated once only when instructional reinforcement is necessary, in classrooms and similar places devoted to instruction within a single building, cluster or campus, as well as in the homes of students receiving formalized home instruction, during the first ten (10) consecutive school days in the forty-five (45) day calendar day retention period. "School days" are school session days – not counting weekends, holidays, vacations, examination periods, or other scheduled interruptions – within the forty-five (45) calendar day retention period.

4. Off-air recordings may be made only at the request of and used by individual teachers, and may not be regularly recorded in anticipation of requests. No broadcast program may be recorded off-air more than once at the request of the same teacher, regardless of the number of times the program may be broadcast.

5. A limited number of copies may be reproduced from each off-air recording to meet the legitimate needs of teachers under these guidelines. Each such additional copy shall be subject to all provisions governing the original recording.

6. After the first ten (10) consecutive school days, off-air recordings may be used up to the end of the forty-five (45) calendar day retention period only for teacher evaluation purposes, i.e., to determine whether or not to include the broadcast program in the teaching curriculum, and may not be used in the recording institution for student exhibition or any other non-evaluation purpose without authorization.

7. Off-air recordings need not be used in their entirety, but the recorded programs may not be altered from their original content. Off-air recordings may not be physically or electronically combined or merged to constitute teaching anthologies or compilations.

8. All copies of off-air recordings must include the copyright notice on the broadcast program as recorded.

9. Educational institutions are expected to establish appropriate control procedures to maintain the integrity of these guidelines.

Appendix E
PRODUCERS: WHO'S (NOT) ENDORSING THE GUIDELINES

The following information is based on replies to a simple questionnaire mailed (except for five Los Angeles–area firms who were con-
tacted by telephone) to approximately 130 producers between
December 1982 and June 1983. The questionnaire asked the name
of the permissions officer and whether or not the organization endorsed the October 1981 off-air educational taping guidelines and
allowed for enclosure of the organization's particular stand or policy regarding educational off-air taping.

Why did so few respond? Eight questionnaires were "returned
to sender"; three reflected media center policy rather than producer's policy; and two indicated that their materials were not
broadcast on TV and therefore were not involved in off-air taping.
This last category may account for several other organizations
that did not respond. As for the rest, there is no clear reason for
their lack of response.

For your convenience, the responding organizations are in one
alphabetical listing, beginning on the next page. Additional information is provided when supplied by the firm. Some firms did not
indicate whether or not they endorsed the guidelines; they simply
sent a copy of their policy, which has been condensed for inclusion
under their listing. The symbols preceding the producers' names
indicate the following: * = endorses guidelines; † = does not endorse guidelines; § = has own policy.

ABC *see* MTI Teleprograms Inc.

*Agency for Instructional Television
Box A
Bloomington, IN 47402
812-339-2203 or 800-457-4509
Contact: Roy Morgan
See Appendix C for joint agreement on school rerecordings; can write for copy of television broadcast policies, procedures, and prices.

†AIMS Media
626 Justin Ave.
Glendale, CA 91201-2398
213-240-9300
Contact: Jerry J. Josten (president)
Licensing fee dependent upon particular request.

AIT *see* Agency for Instructional Television

American Broadcasting Companies see MTI Teleprograms Inc.

*American Humanist Association
7 Harwood Dr.
Amherst, NY 14226
716-839-5080
Contact: Mary C. Murchison-Edwords

†Barr Films
3490 E. Foothill Blvd.
Pasadena, CA 91107
213-793-6153
Contact: John S. Dyas (vice-president)

*Benchmark Films, Inc.
145 Scarborough Rd.
Briarcliff Manor, NY 10510
914-762-3838
Contact: Mike Solin (president)

†BNA Communications Inc.
9417 Decoverly Hall Rd.
Rockville, MD 20850

301-948-0540
Contact: Brigitte Powell

†Bosustow Productions
1649 11th St.
Santa Monica, CA 90404
213-450-3936
Contact: Bernice Coe

†Cally Curtis Co.
1111 N. Las Palmas Ave.
Hollywood, CA 90038
213-467-1101
Contact: Kathy Juden

Centron Films *see* Perspective Films

§Children's Television International, Inc.
8000 Forbes Place (Suite 201)
Springfield, VA 22151
703-321-8455
Contact: Ray Gladfelter (president)
See Appendix C, conditions 1–3; can tape and hold program for length of lease on series.

*Churchill Films
662 N. Robertson Blvd.
Los Angeles, CA 90069
213-657-5110
Contact: Sally Mason

†Concept Media, Inc.
4930 Campus Dr.
Newport Beach, CA 92660
714-833-3347
Contact: Dennis Turley

Coronet Films *see* Perspective Films

†CRM/McGraw-Hill
P.O. Box 641
Del Mar, CA 92014
Contact: Lynn Langley
Product must be purchased before any duplication can be considered.

*DCA Educational Products
424 Valley Rd.
Warrington, PA 18976-2594
215-343-2020
Contact: Bennett V. Schultz (vice-president)

†§EMC Corp.
180 E. Sixth St.
St. Paul, MN 55101
Contact: David E. Feinberg
Each situation subject to specific
negotiations.

†Encyclopaedia Britannica Educational Corp.
425 N. Michigan Ave.
Chicago, IL 60611
312-321-7306
Contact: Harry J. Joy, Jr.
Several licensing plans available,
including annual comprehensive
and annual individual title video
clearance plans; can write for
copy of video policies.

*Faith for Today, Inc.
P.O. Box 320
Newbury Park, CA 91320
805-499-4363
Contact: Don James

*Films Inc.
1144 Wilmette Ave.
Wilmette, IL 60091
312-256-4730
Contact: Television Licensing
Center
Special licensing arrangements
through Television Licensing
Center's clearinghouse.

§Great Plains National Instructional Television Library
Univ. of Nebraska
P.O. Box 80669
Lincoln, NE 68501
402-472-2007 or 800-228-4630
Contact: Stephen C. Lenzen
If school/educational organization
is affiliated with central programming service agency contracting for open-circuit
broadcast of GPN materials:
may record off air and reuse for
balance of school year; can only
be used within school/educational organization, i.e., cannot
be sold, loaned, etc.; must be
erased at end of school year
unless multiyear contract; some
instances of off-air recording
restrictions due to distribution
rights.

†Handel Film Corp.
8730 Sunset Blvd.
W. Hollywood, CA 90069
213-657-8990
Contact: Leo A. Handel
(president)
Duplication rights not included
with purchase

†Journal Films, Inc.
930 Pitner Ave.
Evanston, IL 60202
312-328-6700
Contact: Anne Reardon
Provides 7-day convenience rights
at no charge to schools served
by ETV/ITV stations acquiring
the programs; for duplication or
off-air rights, write for fee
schedule.

LCA Video/Films see Learning
Corp. of America

†Learning Corp. of America
1350 Ave. of the Americas
New York, NY 10019
212-397-9330
Contact: Elaine Mason

†McGraw-Hill Films
1221 Ave. of the Americas
New York, NY 10020
212-997-6168
Contact: Josephine Chessare

§**The Media Guild**
118 S. Acacia Ave.
P.O. Box 881
Solana Beach, CA 92075
714-755-9191
Contact: James LeMay
Duplication licenses available; can write for duplication policy.

†**MTI Teleprograms Inc.**
3710 Commercial Ave.
Northbrook, IL 60062
800-323-5343
IL, AK, HI: 312-291-9400 (call collect)
Licensing arrangements available.

***National Council of Churches (Communication Commission)**
475 Riverside Dr.
New York, NY 10115
212-870-2574
Contact: Dave Pomeroy

†**National Educational Media, Inc.**
21061 Devonshire St.
Chatsworth, CA 91311
213-709-6009
Contact: Jack L. Copeland (president)

†**National Geographic Society (Educational Services)**
17th and M Streets, N.W.
Washington, DC 20036
202-857-7000
Contact: Wendy C. Rogers (manager)
Encourages use of its preview agency: Karol Media, 625 From Rd., Paramus, NJ 07652. 201-262-4170.

***PBS Video**
475 L'Enfant Plaza, S.W.
Washington, DC 20024
202-488-5220 or 800-424-7963
Contact: Rosemary Schommer

***Perennial Education, Inc.**
477 Roger Williams Ave.
Highland Park, IL 60035
312-433-1610 or 800-323-9084
Contact: Nancy Ries

†**Perspective Films**
65 E. South Water St.
Chicago, IL 60601
800-621-2131
Contact: John Creeden
Permission needed; licensing arrangements available.

Public Media Inc. *see* Films Inc.

Public Television Library *see* PBS Video

†**Pyramid Films**
P.O. Box 1048
Santa Monica, CA 90406
213-828-7577
Contact: Jim Bochneak
Licensing arrangements available.

†**Ramic Productions, Inc.**
(4910 Birch St.)
P.O. Box 7530
Newport Beach, CA 92660
714-833-2444 or 800-854-0223
Contact: Charles Dexter

†**Ramsgate Films**
704 Santa Monica Blvd.
Santa Monica, CA 90401
213-394-8819
Contact: Vaughn Obern

†**Roundtable Films Inc.**
113 N. San Vicente Blvd.
Beverly Hills, CA 90211
213-657-1402
Contact: Ken Newelt

†**Salenger Educational Media**
1635 12th St.
Santa Monica, CA 90404
213-450-1300
Contact: Fred Salenger

*Science Software Systems, Inc.
11899 W. Pico Blvd.
Los Angeles, CA 90064
213-477-8541
Contact: Richard A. Boolootian

†Vantage Communications Inc.
P.O. Box 546
Nyack, NY 10960
914-358-0147
Contact: Roger W. Seiler

†Walt Disney Educational Media
  Co.
500 S. Buena Vista St.
Burbank, CA 91521

213-840-1111
Contact: Richard P. Boehning

*Western Instructional Television,
  Inc.
1438 N. Gower St.
Los Angeles, CA 90028
213-466-8601
Contact: Donna Matson

†Xicom-Video Arts Film Produc-
  tions
Serling Forest
Tuxedo, NY 10987
914-351-4735
Contact: Arthur J. Blazek

Appendix F
GLOSSARY

Every effort has been made to present the information in this book in "everyday" language. However, as the language of the legal field may prove a hindrance to a ready understanding of the issues, the following definitions are provided for the reader's convenience.*

Action. A legal proceeding (strictly speaking, at common law) to enforce one's rights against another.

Affirm. To declare that a lower court judgment, decree, or order is valid and legally correct even if the reasoning behind the judgment is rejected.

Appeal. An application by an *appellant* to a higher court to rectify an order of a lower court.

Appellant. The losing party in a lower court ruling who takes the case to the next level of the courts for review. The opposing party is called the *appellee* or *respondent.* See also *petitioner.*

Appellate court. A court of appeal, that is, not the court where the case was first heard. The U.S. Supreme Court is the ultimate court of appeal.

Appellee. Sometimes called *respondent,* this is the party against whom the appeal is made; that is, this party does not want the court to reverse or set aside the judgment. Status as appellant or appellee does not necessarily correspond to the lower court status of *plaintiff* or *defendant.* The opposing party is called *appellant.*

Case. Any proceeding in law contested before a court.

Case law. The body of law developed by case decisions.

Certiorari. Based on a petition to an appellate court, a plea or an order, when granted, for a lower court to "certify" its record of a particular case and send it up to the appellate court for review. The appellate court may

*The primary sources used to establish these definitions were *Black's Law Dictionary,* 5th edition (Black, 1979); *Words and Phrases* (West, n.d.); and the glossary of legal terms provided in *The Law and the College Student: Justice in Evolution* (Millington, 1979).

grant or deny certiorari (that is, agree or refuse to review the case) as it sees fit, without stating its reasons.

Citation. Legal reference to a case indicating (in the order it is read) the plaintiff, defendant, volume number, publication, page number, and year the case was decided.

Common law. Law continually developing through court decisions as opposed to statutes and regulations.

Constructive knowledge. Basically, the idea that ignorance of the law is not an excuse. If a person, exercising reasonable care, would have known a fact because it was, for example, a matter of public record, then he or she can be held responsible.

Copyright. The right of literary property granted by statute to an author or originator of certain literary works or artistic productions. For a limited time, the author or originator is invested with exclusive production and distribution rights. This right does not extend to an idea, procedure, process, system, method of operation, concept, principle, or discovery.

Copyright Act. The revised Copyright Act of 1976 – Public Law 94-553, 90 Stat. 2541 (1976), Title 17 of the U.S. Code codified at 17 U.S.C. Sections 101-810 [1976] – which took effect on January 1, 1978. All references to code section numbers are to this law. Its predecessor is usually referred to as the Copyright Act of 1909.

Declaratory judgment. Statutory remedy for determination of justiciable controversy where plaintiff is in doubt as to his legal rights; binding adjudication of rights and status of litigants even though no consequential relief is awarded.

Defendant. The party against whom the lawsuit is brought.

De minimus. Insufficient injury to support a cause of action.

Dissenting opinion. A judge's explicit disagreement with the majority opinion.

Enumerated power. Powers specifically granted to the federal government by the Constitution.

Equitable estoppel. Doctrine by which a person may be precluded by his act, conduct, or silence – when it is his duty to speak – from asserting a right that otherwise would be his.

Equity. Justice administered by fairness rather than strictly formulated rules of common law.

Estoppel. An inconsistent position or attitude may not be adopted to the loss or injury of another.

Fair use. The privilege, in other than the copyright owner, to use copyrighted material in a reasonable manner without the owner's consent, notwithstanding the monopoly granted to the owner. The 1976 Copyright Act set forth four factors for determining whether the use made of a work in any particular case is a fair one.

Injunction. A prohibitive, equitable remedy granted by the court at the suit of the complainant and directed to the defendant in the action. It forbids the defendant from doing some act, or restrains the defendant from continuing such an act, because the act is judged unjust, unequitable, injurious to the plaintiff, and not adequately redressed by an action at law.

Laches. Based upon the maxim that equity aids the vigilant and not those who slumber on their rights; neglect to assert right or claim; operates as bar in court of equity.

Majority opinion. The statement of reasons for a decision agreed to by a majority of the appellate court judges when the court is not unanimous.

Minority opinion. The statement of reasons given by the appellate court judges who do not agree with the majority opinion. If these judges do not agree on the reasons for their disapproval, they usually write separate dissenting opinions.

Off-air videotaping. Or, off-air videotape recording; the electronic reproduction of the television signal at the time of broadcast onto a blank videotape.

Petitioner. Party presenting a petition to a court, either to start *equity* proceeding or appeal from a judgment. The party opposing the petition, that is, the party against whom action or relief is desired, is the *respondent*. See also *appellant* and *appellee*.

Plaintiff. The one who initiates the lawsuit.

Prima facie At first sight; on the face of it; presumed to be true.

Public access. The freest possible dissemination of information for the benefit of society.

Res judicata. A decided case; a matter already settled.

Respondent. The party opposing the appeal, that is, the *appellee*. In *equity*, the party answering the equity proceeding.

Appendix G
QUICK REFERENCE*

1. What is copyright?
   It is an enumerated power designed to advance the public welfare by promoting artistic and scientific progress.

2. What is the current Copyright Act?
   The current act is PL 94-553, 90 Stat. 2541, Title 17 of the *U.S. Code.* It was passed in 1976 and went into effect on January 1, 1978.

3. What can be copyrighted?
   Original works in any tangible medium of expression (Section 102).

4. Is there anything that cannot be copyrighted?
   The following cannot be copyrighted: an idea, procedure, process, system, method of operation, concept, principle, or discovery (Section 102).

5. What is the idea–expression dichotomy?
   It is one way the courts reconcile public access and economic reward to the creator. Since an idea cannot be copyrighted, the public can benefit and progress from using it. Since the expression used to convey the idea is copyrightable, the creator can receive recompense for that particular expression of the idea.

6. Are unpublished works protected by copyright?
   Yes, without regard to author's nationality or domicile (Section 104[a]).

*First published in *Instructional Innovator* (January, 1984, pp. 44 and 47) and reprinted with the kind permission of *Instructional Innovator.*

7. Are works of the U.S. government copyrightable?
No (Section 105). But, works funded by the government but developed by private individuals may be copyrightable.

8. What are the copyright owner's exclusive rights?
Subject to Sections 107–118, a copyright owner has the exclusive right to reproduce copies, prepare derivative works, distribute copies, perform publicly, and display publicly the copyrighted work (Section 106).

9. How long does a copyright last?
Under the current Act, a copyright exists for the life of the author plus 50 years (Section 302).

10. What is fair use?
Fair use allows someone other than the copyright owner to use a work without permission. It originated in the courts as a means of balancing the copyright owner's exclusive rights when those rights would inhibit the dissemination of information. It remained a judicial limitation on copyright exclusivity until its appearance as Section 107 of the present Copyright Act. The four key criteria of fair use are (1) the purpose and character of use; (2) the nature of the copyrighted work; (3) the amount used; and (4) the effect of the use on the market value (present or future) of the work.

11. Aren't fair use and educational use synonymous?
No. Section 107 gives six examples of fair use: criticism, comment, news reporting, teaching, scholarship, and research. The first three are traditionally accepted as fair use. The remaining three have not always been accepted as fair use. Teaching was included due to educational lobbying efforts. Thus, an educational use may be considered fair use, depending on the specific circumstances of the use.

12. Does the Copyright Act itself allow off-the-air taping?
The Act itself only allows a library or archives to tape "an audiovisual news program" (Section 108 [f] [3]). This clause was included to help resolve the CBS v. Vanderbilt suits.

13. What are the current educational off-air taping guidelines?
These are suggested educational fair use standards negotiated by the concerned parties and included in the legislative history of the current Copyright Act. Since they are part of the legislative history, they do not have the force of law. Furthermore, they do not cover every possible activity, are subject to future review, and do not always represent all of the concerned parties.

14. To whom do the guidelines apply?
    Nonprofit educational institutions.

15. Are libraries included in the guidelines?
    Yes and no. Yes if it is a school or academic library serving the instructional media needs of the teachers and students. No if it is a for-profit library. Unless a public library directly serves a particular nonprofit educational institution's instructional needs, it would also seem to fall outside the scope of the guidelines. Libraries are, however, allowed to tape the news (Section 108 [f] [3]).

16. What is meant by "broadcast programs"?
    TV programs transmitted for reception by the general public without charge.

17. Can a program be taped off-air from a cable station?
    Yes and no. Yes if the program is being simultaneously re-transmitted by a cable system. No if the program is being shown on, for example, pay cable, pay TV, or Instructional Television Fixed Service.

18. How long can a tape (made off the air) be retained?
    According to the guidelines, for 45 consecutive calendar days. After that, they must be erased.

19. Can a school build a library of its off-the-air tapes?
    Not unless licenses or permissions have been obtained that extend the 45-day guideline retention period. Otherwise, the school will find itself liable for copyright infringement.

20. Can the tapes be shown to the class at any time during the 45-day retention period?
    No. The tape can be used for instructional purposes only during the first ten consecutive school days. The remaining time is for teacher evaluation of its instructional usefulness in the curriculum.

21. How often can a teacher use the tapes during the ten-day period?
    Only once in each class. However, if instructional reinforcement is deemed necessary, a repeat showing is allowed.

22. If a program was recorded right before summer vacation, can it be kept over the summer for use at the start of the fall semester?
    No. The 45-day retention period would have expired before the start of the fall semester. The tape should have been erased during the summer.

23. Can a tape be made in anticipation of teacher requests?
No. Off-air recordings may be made only upon the request of individual teachers.

24. What happens if several teachers request taping of the same program?
The guidelines allow for some copies of the off-air recording to be made to meet legitimate teacher needs. Each copy is governed by the guidelines.

25. If a program was taped during the fall semester for one teacher, can it be taped during the spring semester for another teacher?
Yes. The guidelines only prohibit the same teacher from requesting that a program be taped more than once.

26. Can specific segments from a program be used or must the entire program be shown?
Specific segments can be used as long as the original content is not altered.

27. Does the use of the guidelines preclude the need for a license or letter of permission to tape a TV broadcast?
No. According to the negotiating committee's letter to Representative Kastenmeier, specific licenses and permissions may still be required. In addition, many producers did not endorse the guidelines, and their programs, therefore, might not be covered by the guidelines.

28. Since many TV programs are broadcast outside of school hours, would it be permissible for a teacher to tape the program at home as long as it was for school use as per the guidelines?
There is some support indicating that such taping would be within the guidelines if this did not become systematic copying and the guidelines were followed in all else.

29. Can a school district or regional cooperative record off-air, duplicate, and distribute tapes to all the schools under its jurisdiction?
NO. BOCES did just that and lost all three of the court decisions. Systematic and/or large-scale off-air taping is considered a copyright infringement.

30. Can a school district or regional cooperative tape off-air for temporary uses?
According to the most recent *BOCES* decision (1983), the answer is no. However, the court noted its decision was limited specifically to this case.

31. If an infringement is found, how much will it cost the infringer?

There is no one answer. A copyright owner is entitled to actual damages and any profits made on the infringement. If statutory damages are applied, the infringer can be liable for $250 to $10,000. However, if the infringer believed his or her copying was under Section 107 (for example, an employee of a nonprofit, educational institution or library), "the court shall remit statutory damages" (Section 504).

CHAPTER REFERENCES
AND BIBLIOGRAPHY

ADDITIONAL REFERENCES

Chapter 1

Beard (1974), Blackwell (1974), Bugbee (1967), Callison (1981), Chafee (1945b), Clapp (1968), Clark (1979–1980), Cohen, S. (1969), Deely (1976), Diamond (1975), "Education and copyright" (1970), Fields (1982b), Gilkey (1969/1972), Goldstein (1970), Golub (1977), Gordon, R. (1981), Greguras (1981), Hart, W. (1981), Hattery (1972), Hayes (1978), Henry (1975), Holland (1978), Howell (1979), Johnson (1981), Katz, A. S. (1977), Keyes (1980), Kies (1975, 1980), Koenig (1980), Krasilovsky (1969), Kunzle (1980), Latman (1958/1963, 1977), Lawrence (1980a), "Lawsuit involving" (1983), Liekweg (1979), Marke (1977), Meade (1967), Miller, P. C. (1979), Munshi (1980), Patterson (1968), Peters (1979), "Publishers file" (1982), Purdy (1980), "Registrar issues" (1983), Ringer (1968/1972), Roberts (1980), Robinson (1981), Saettler (1968), Saunders (1972), Seltzer (1978), "Squibb settles" (1982), Stern (1981), Stork (1972), Streibich (1975), "Symposium" (1977), Taubman (1977), Timberg, B. (1980), Troost (1976, 1977, 1978b), Tseng (1979), U.S. Copyright Office (1977–1978), Wincor (1962).

Chapter 2

Copeland (1983), Crabb (1976), Fields (1982a), "Home recording" (1982), "King report" (1982), "Response of the ALA" (1982), Roth (1982), Ruark (1983), Troost (1983), Watson (1983), "WIPO conference" (1983), Zemke (1983).

Chapter 3

"AECT acts" (1982), American Library Association (1981), Bender (1982), Best (1977), "Betamax" case" (1983), Breyer (1972), Brittin (1982), Chambers (1939), Chee (1977), Choate & Francis (1981), Cohen, M. L.

(1978), "Copyright fair use" (1969), Eaton (1977), Glover (1982), Goldstein (1970), Goldwag (1979), Good & Scates (1954), Hans (1979), Hart, B. (1975), Hoard (1978), "Home taping" (1983), "Home-video case" (1983), Hurt & Schuchman (1966), "Independent creativity" (1982), Isaac & Michael (1971), Kaplan & Brown (1978), Katz, A. E. (1977), Kerlinger (1973), Kutner (1967), Lawrence, M. S. (1982), Meyer (1971), Miller, J. K. (1982), Mowrey (1982), Nimmer (1979), Oakes (1978), Palmer (1983), "Petitioners in 'Betamax' " (1982), Ringer (1977a), Rosenfield (1980), Simkin & Weinberg (1981), Sullivan (1977), "Supreme Court agrees" (1982), "TV taping" (1984), Tyerman (1971/1974), Van Dalen (1979), "Videotaping of copyrighted" (1982), Zissu (1980).

Chapter 4

Copeland (1984), Crook (1982a, 1982b), Gordon, P. C. (1982), Greenspan (1982), Harris (1982), Hoffman (1982), MacLean (1972), Schwartz (1982), Stewart (1966), Young (1982).

BOOKS, ARTICLES, AND LEGISLATIVE MATERIALS

AECT [Association for Educational Communications & Technology] acts as *amicus curiae* in Sony case. *ECT Network*, July–August 1982, *1*(5), 1.

Aleinikoff, E. N. Fair use and broadcasting. In J. S. Lawrence & B. Timberg (Eds.), *Fair use and free inquiry: Copyright law and the new media.* Norwood, N.J.: Ablex, 1980.

American Library Association. Brief amicus curiae in support of the petition for writ of certiorari to the United States Court of Appeals for the Ninth Circuit. *Universal* v. *Sony,* October 1981.

American Library Association. *The new copyright law: Questions teachers & librarians ask.* Washington, D.C.: NEA, 1977.

Arié, M. L. Author's rights (le droit d'auteur) and contemporary audiovisual techniques in France. In J. S. Lawrence & B. Timberg (Eds.), *Fair use and free inquiry: Copyright law and the new media.* Norwood, N.J.: Ablex, 1980.

Association for Educational Communications & Technology. *Copyright and educational media: A guide to fair use and permissions procedure.* Washington, D.C.: Author, 1977. (a)

Association for Educational Communications & Technology. *Copyright: New law, new directions.* Washington, D.C.: Author, 1977. (Filmstrip) (b)

Association of Media Producers. *Directory of rights & permissions officers.* Washington, D.C.: Author, n.d.

At last (whew)! Off-air copying guidelines. *Instructional Innovator,* September 1981, *26*(6), 36–37.

Ball, H. G. *The law of copyright and literary property.* Albany, N.Y.: M. Bender, 1944.

Beard, J. J. The copyright issue. *Annual Review of Information Science and Technology,* 1974, *9*, 381–411.

Beard, J. J. The sale, rental, and reproduction of motion picture videocassettes: Piracy or privilege? *New England Law Review,* 1979–80, *15*, 435–484.

Bender, I. The legal copy. *TLC Guide,* 1980, *1*(2), 7–8.

Bender, I. BOCES decision: Guilty. *TLC Guide,* 1982, *3*(2), 8.

Best, J. W. *Research in education* (3rd ed.). Englewood Cliffs, N.J.: Prentice-Hall, 1977.

"Betamax" case argued before Supreme Court. *Patent, Trademark & Copyright Journal,* 1983, *25*, 227–229.

Bill would legalize in-home videotaping. *Patent, Trademark & Copyright Journal,* October 22, 1981, p. AA-2.

Billings, R. D. Off-the-air videorecording, face-to-face teaching, and the 1976 Copyright Act. *Northern Kentucky Law Review,* 1977, *4*, 225–251.

Bistline, S. The snarls are still there. *Media & Methods,* October 1977, *14*(2), 36–38.

Black, H. C. *Black's law dictionary* (5th ed.). St. Paul, Minn.: West, 1979.

Blackwell, T. E. The law of copyright and the fair use doctrine. *The Journal of College and University Law,* 1974, *1*, 222–229.

Bloom, H. S. The copyright position in Britain. In J. S. Lawrence & B. Timberg (Eds.), *Fair use and free inquiry: Copyright law and the new media.* Norwood, N.J.: Ablex, 1980.

Boorstin, D. *The image.* New York: Harper & Row, 1964.

Brennan, T. C. Legislative history and chapter 1 of S.22. In New York Law School Law Review, *The complete guide to the new copyright law.* New York: Lorenz Press, 1977. (Originally published, *New York Law School Law Review,* 1976, *22*.)

Breyer, S. The uneasy case for copyright: A study of copyright in books, photocopies, and computer programs. *Harvard Law Review,* 1970, *84*, 281–351.

Breyer, S. Copyright: A rejoinder. *UCLA Law Review,* 1972, *20*, 75–83.

Brittin, M. D. Constitutional fair use. *William & Mary Law Review,* 1978, *20*, 85–123.

Brittin, M. D. Constitutional fair use. *American Society of Composers, Authors and Publishers Copyright Law Symposium,* 1982, *28*, 141–188.

Bugbee, B. W. *Genesis of American patent and copyright law.* Washington, D.C.: Public Affair Press, 1967.

Callison, D. Fair payment for fair use in future information technology systems. *Educational Technology,* January 1981, *21* (1), 20–25.

Cambridge Research Institute. *Omnibus copyright revision: Comparative analysis of the issues.* Washington, D.C.: American Society for Information Science, 1973.

Cardozo, M. H. To copy or not to copy for teaching and scholarship: What shall I tell my client? *The Journal of College and University Law,* 1976–1977, *4,* 59–81.

Chafee, Z., Jr. Reflections on the law of copyright: I. *Columbia Law Review,* 1945, *45,* 503–529. (a)

Chafee, Z., Jr. Reflections on the law of copyright: II. *Columbia Law Review,* 1945, *45,* 719–734. (b)

Chambers, M. M. Legal research in education. *Review of Educational Research,* December 1939, *9,* 460–465; 594–595.

Chee, L. How to research copyright law. *Law Library Journal,* 1977, *70,* 171–183.

Choate, R. A., & Francis, W. H. *Cases and materials on patent law, also including trade secrets – copyrights – trademarks* (2nd ed.). St. Paul, Minn.: West, 1981.

Churchill, R. The unauthorized reproduction of educational audiovisual materials – golden egg production: The goose cries "foul." In J. S. Lawrence & B. Timberg (Eds.), *Fair use and free inquiry: Copyright law and the new media.* Norwood, N.J.: Ablex, 1980.

Clapp. V. W. *Copyright – a librarian's view.* Washington, D.C.: Association of Research Libraries, 1968.

Clark, C. R. *Universal City Studios, Inc.* v. *Sony Corporation of America:* Application of the fair use doctrine under the United States Copyright Acts of 1909 and 1976. *New England Law Review,* 1979–1980, *15,* 661–681.

Cocks, J. Crackdown in the living room. *Time,* November 2, 1981, *118*(18), 70.

Cohen, M. L. *Legal research in a nutshell* (3rd ed.). St. Paul, Minn.: West, 1978.

Cohen, S. Fair use in the law of copyright. *American Society of Composers, Authors and Publishers Copyright Law Symposium,* 1955, *6,* 43–71.

Cohen, S. Primitive copyright. *American Bar Association Journal,* 1969, *55,* 1144–1147.

Cooke, E. Off-air copying update: Guidelines, advice to educators. *American Libraries,* December 1981, *12,* 663–664.

Copeland, J. Letter to the editor. *Training,* June 1983, *20*(6), 14.

Copeland, J. Personal communication. January 1984.

Copyright controversy continued. *ECT,* June 1981, *11*(8), 2.

Copyright fair use – case law and legislation. *Duke Law Journal,* 1969, *1969,* 73–109.

Crabb, G. Copyright and its relevance in education. *Visual Education,* March 1976, pp. 19; 21–22.

Crook, D. Just who's right on the home taping issue? *Los Angeles Times,* April 12, 1982, Pt. IV, pp. 1; 8. (a)

Crook, D. Two sides to blank tape. *Los Angeles Times,* April 16, 1982, Pt. VI, pp. 1; 8. (b)

Crossland, H. J. The rise and fall of fair use: The protection of literary materials against copyright infringement by new and developing media. *South Carolina Law Review,* 1968, *20,* 153–242.

Current developments in CATV. New York: Practising Law Institute, 1981.

Deely, P. Copyright: Limitation on exclusive rights, fair use. *Houston Law Review,* 1976, *13,* 1041–1061.

DeFelice, H. L. Copyright: Gone with the Betamax? *New York University Review of Law and Social Change,* 1978–1979, *8,* 45–62.

Diamond, S. A. Videotape, piracy & the law. *Audio-Visual Communication,* July 1975, *9*(7), 10–11; 27.

Does the showing of videocassette tapes of motion pictures to prison inmates by correctional authorities constitute an infringement of copyright? 65 Ops. Cal. Atty. Gen. 106 (1982).

Duemmler, F. L. Library photocopying: An international perspective. *American Society of Composers, Authors and Publishers Copyright Law Symposium,* 1981, *26,* 151–196.

Eaton, J. W. Copyright – originality – confusing the standards for granting copyrights and patents. *West Virginia Law Review,* 1977, *79,* 410–422.

Education and copyright law: An analysis of the amended copyright revision bill and proposal for statutory licensing and a clearinghouse system. *Virginia Law Review,* 1970, *56,* 664–689.

Educational group not entitled to limited copying under "fair use." *Patent, Trademark & Copyright Journal,* 1983, *25,* 501–503.

English, E. Personal communication, March 3, 1982.

Essman, P. Personal communication, April 1980.

Federal judge rules temporary educational use of videotape copies of copyrighted works illegal. *Phi Delta Kappan,* June 1983, *64,* 746.

A few words about the Television Licensing Center. *TLC Guide,* October 15, 1980, *1*(2), 2.

Fields, H. Copyright Office report shows low photocopying payments. *Publishers Weekly,* 1982, *221*(24), 14; 19. (a)

Fields, H. AAP to sue "large eastern university." *Publishers Weekly,* 1982, *222*(24), 16. (b)

Finkelstein, H. ASCAP as an example of the clearing house system in operation. *Bulletin of the Copyright Society of the U.S.A.,* 1966, *14,* 2–7.

Freid, S. Fair use and the new act. In New York Law School Law Review, *The complete guide to the new copyright law.* New York: Lorenz Press, 1977. (Originally published, *New York Law School Law Review,* 1977, *22.*)

Fritch, B. E. Some copyright implications of videotapes. *American Society of Composers, Authors and Publishers Copyright Law Symposium,* 1964, *13,* 87–132.

Gilkey, R. Instructional media copyright: Technology, ethics, and instruction. In G. P. Bush (Ed.), *Technology and copyright: Annotated bibliography and source materials.* Mt. Airy, Md.: Lomond System, 1972. (Reprinted from *The Clearing House,* December 1969, *44.*)

Glover, J. S. Betamax and copyright: The home videorecording controversy. *American Society of Composers, Authors and Publishers Copyright Law Symposium,* 1982, *28,* 235–271.

Goldstein, P. Copyright and the first amendment. *Columbia Law Review,* 1970, *70,* 983–1057.

Goldwag, C. Copyright infringement and the first amendment. *Columbia Law Review,* 1979, *79,* 320–340.

Golub, M. V. Not by books alone: Library copying of nonprint, copyright material. *Law Library Journal,* 1977, *70,* 153–170.

Good, C. V., & Scates, D. E. *Methods of research.* New York: Appleton-Century-Crofts, 1954.

Gordon, P. C. Feedback: Copyright guidelines, round 2. *Instructional Innovator,* September 1982, *27*(6), 13.

Gordon, R. Program writers get expanded protection. *Computer Careers News,* January 12, 1981, *2*(1), 3.

Greenspan, E. A man's cassette is his castle: A home use exemption from copyright infringement? *American Society of Composers, Authors and Publishers Copyright Law Symposium,* 1982, *28,* 189–234.

Greguras, F. M. A new look at patentability. *Mini-Micro Systems,* June 1981, *14*(6), 161; 163–164.

Gross, L. S. Copyrights and pragmatism. *Educational Broadcasting,* September–October 1975, *8*(5), 19–20; 37.

Grossman, B. A. Cycles in copyright. In New York Law School Law Review, *The complete guide to the new copyright law.* New York: Lorenz Press, 1977. (Originally published, *New York Law School Law Review,* 1977, *22.*)

Hans, P. E. Constitutional law – commercial speech – copyright and the first amendment. *Wisconsin Law Review,* 1979, *1979,* 242–266.

Harris, K. Royalties backed for tapings made at home. *Los Angeles Times,* April 13, 1982, Pt. IV, pp. 1; 12.

Hart, B. Copyrights: Concurrence, revision, and photocopying — *Williams & Wilkins Company* v. *United States,* a "holding operation" by the United States Court of Claims. *Dickinson Law Review,* 1975, *79,* 260-308.

Hart, R. M., & Schuchman, R. M. The economic rationale of copyright. *American Economic Review,* 1966, *56,* 421-432.

Hart, W. M. The conscientious fair user's guide to the Copyright Act of 1976: Video recordation and its fair use. *University of Pittsburg Law Review,* 1981, *42,* 317-374.

Hattery, L. H. Foreword. In G. P. Bush (Ed.), *Technology and copyright: Annotated bibliography and source materials.* Mt. Airy, Md.: Lomond Systems, 1972.

Hayes, D. J. Classroom "fair use": A reevaluation. *Bulletin of the Copyright Society of the U.S.A.,* 1978, *26,* 101-129.

Heinemann, K., & Troost, F. W. California Media and Library Educators Association position regarding off-air video tape copying of televised broadcasts. *CMLEA Journal,* 1979, Spring-Summer, *2,* 1-4.

Henn, H. G. Cassandra considers copyright. *Bulletin of the Copyright Society of the U.S.A.,* 1978, *25,* 453-472.

Henry. N. *Copyright — information technology — public policy* (2 vols.). New York: Marcel Dekker, 1975.

Herring, B. G. Library and learning resources: How will copyright apply? In J. S. Lawrence & B. Timberg (Eds.), *Fair use and free inquiry: Copyright law and the new media.* Norwood, N.J.: Ablex, 1980.

Hoard, S. L. Copyright law — one step beyond fair use: A direct public interest qualification premised on the first amendment. *North Carolina Law Review,* 1978, *57,* 150-163.

Hoffman, D. Feedback: Copyright guidelines, round 1. *Instructional Innovator,* September 1982, *27*(6), 11-13.

Holland, M. J. A brief history of American copyright law. In H. S. White (Ed.), *The copyright dilemma.* Chicago: ALA, 1978.

Home recording of copyrighted works. *ALA Washington Newsletter,* 1982, *34*(10), 1-9.

Home taping of TV shows stays in legal limbo. *Los Angeles Times,* July 6, 1983, p. 1.

Home-video case ordered rerun by Supreme Court. *Wall Street Journal,* July 7, 1983, p.8.

Howell, H. A. *Copyright law: Howell's copyright law revised and the 1976 act* (5th ed., A. Latman, Ed.). Washington, D.C.: Bureau of National Affairs, 1979.

How to become a TLC member. *TLC Guide,* February 1, 1981, *1*(4), 10.

Hutchins, R. M. *The higher learning in America.* New Haven: Yale University Press, 1936.

Independent creativity is key to fair use defense, "Betamax" respondents say. *Patent, Trademark & Copyright Journal,* 1982, *25,* 97–98.

Isaac, S., & Michael, W. B. *Handbook in research and evaluation.* San Diego: EdITS, 1971.

Jeremiah. In H. Freedman (Ed.), *Soncino books of the Bible.* London: Soncino Press, 1961.

Johnson, K. Software copyright protection. *Data Base Monthly,* April 1981, pp. 14–15.

Johnston, D. F. *Copyright handbook.* New York: Bowker, 1978.

Johnston, D. F. Exclusive rights of copyright, fair use; reproduction by libraries; effect of transfer of particular copy of phonorecord. *Current Developments in Copyright Law,* 1980, pp. 93–203.

Jones, T. S. Copyright: An overview. *Oklahoma City University Law Review,* 1979, *3,* 713–722.

Kadden, R. S. Copyright law. *1978 Annual Survey of American Law,* 1979, pp. 593–629.

Kallal, E. W., Jr. Betamax and infringement of television copyright. *Duke Law Journal,* 1978, *1977,* 1181–1218.

Kaplan, B. *An unhurried view of copyright.* New York: Columbia University Press, 1967.

Kaplan, B., & Brown, R. S., Jr. *Cases on copyright, unfair competition, and other topics bearing on the protection of literary, musical, and artistic works* (3rd ed.). Mineola, N.Y.: The Foundation Press, 1978.

Katz, A. E. The general revision of the copyright law — from bare bones to corpulence – a partial overview. *Pepperdine Law Review,* 1977, *4,* 213–241.

Katz, A. S. The 1976 Copyright Revision Act and authors' rights: A negative overview. *Pepperdine Law Review,* 1977, *4,* 171–212.

Kellner, D. Television research and fair use. In J. S. Lawrence & B. Timberg (Eds.), *Fair use and free inquiry: Copyright law and the new media.* Norwood, N.J.: Ablex, 1980.

Kerlinger, F. N. *Foundations of behavioral research* (2nd ed.). New York: Holt, Rinehart and Winston, 1973.

Keyes, A. A. Copyright and fair dealing in Canada. In J. S. Lawrence & B. Timberg (Eds.), *Fair use and free inquiry: Copyright law and the new media.* Norwood, N.J.: Ablex, 1980.

Kies, C. Copyright versus free access: CBS and Vanderbilt University square off. *Wilson Library Bulletin,* November 1975, *50,* 242–246.

Kies, C. The CBS-Vanderbilt litigation: Taping the evening news. In J. S. Lawrence & B. Timberg (Eds.), *Fair use and free inquiry: Copyright law and the new media.* Norwood, N.J.: Ablex, 1980.

King Report on copyright reinforces ALA stand. *American Libraries,* July–August 1982, *13*(7), 445.

Klaver, F. The legal problems of video-cassettes and audio-visual discs. *Bulletin of the Copyright Society of the U.S.A.,* 1976, *23,* 152–185.

Koenig, C. F. Software copyright: The conflict within CONTU. *Bulletin of the Copyright Society of the U.S.A.,* 1980, *27,* 340–378.

Krasilovsky, M. W. The effect of copyright practices on educational innovation. *The Record-Teachers College,* 1969, *70,* 413–427.

Kunzle, D. Hogarth piracies and the origin of visual copyright. In J. S. Lawrence & B. Timberg (Eds.), *Fair use and free inquiry: Copyright law and the new media.* Norwood, N.J.: Ablex, 1980.

Kutner, L. The neglected ninth amendment: The "other rights" retained by the people. *Marquette Law Review,* 1967, *51,* 121–142.

Latman, A. Fair use of copyrighted works. In The Copyright Society of the U.S.A., *Studies on copyright* (Arthur Fisher Memorial Edition, vol. 2). South Hackensack, N.J.: Fred B. Rothman, 1963. (Reprinted from Copyright Office Study No. 14, 1958.)

Latman, A. Copyright law. *1976 Annual Survey of American Law,* 1977, 629–648.

Lawrence, J. S. Copyright law, fair use, and the academy: An introduction. In J. S. Lawrence & B. Timberg (Eds.), *Fair use and free inquiry: Copyright law and the new media.* Norwood, N.J.: Ablex, 1980. (a)

Lawrence, J. S. Donald Duck v. Chilean socialism: A fair use exchange. In J. S. Lawrence & B. Timberg (Eds.), *Fair use and free inquiry: Copyright law and the new media.* Norwood, N.J.: Ablex, 1980. (b)

Lawrence, M. S. Fair use: Evidence of change in a traditional doctrine. *American Society of Composers, Authors and Publishers Copyright Law Symposium,* 1982, *27,* 71–112.

Lawsuit involving photocopying for educational purposes is settled. *Patent, Trademark & Copyright Journal,* 1983, *25,* 483–484.

Lee, D. M. Personal communication, November 19, 1981.

Lee, J. W., & Laterza, N. R. Educators, fair use, and the new act: All concerned are not protected. *The University of Toledo Law Review,* 1977, *9,* 130–151.

Libraries, publishers and photocopying: Final report of surveys conducted for the United States Copyright Office. Rockville, Md.: King Research, 1982.

Liekweg, J. A. New copyright law and its implications. *The Catholic Lawyer,* 1979, *24,* 210–216.

McDonald, J. A. Non-infringing uses. *Bulletin of the Copyright Society of the U.S.A.,* 1962, *9,* 466–471.

MacLean, A. W. Education and copyright law: An analysis of the amended copyright revision bill and proposals for statutory licensing and a clearinghouse system. *American Society of Composers, Authors and Publishers Copyright Law Symposium*, 1972, *20*, 1–35.

Madison, J. General view of the powers proposed to be vested in the Union: The same view continued (Essay 43). In A. Hamilton, J. Madison, & J. Jay (Eds.), *The federalist papers*. New York: Mentor Books, 1961. (Originally published, 1788.)

Magarrell, J. "Exaggerated" warnings inhibit legal use of printed materials, Copyright Office told. *The Chronicle of Higher Education*, October 20, 1980, *21*(9), 21.

Marke, J. J. United States copyright revision and its legislative history. *Law Library Journal*, 1977, *70*, 121–152.

Mast, G. Film study and the copyright law. In J. S. Lawrence & B. Timberg (Eds.), *Fair use and free inquiry: Copyright law and the new media*. Norwood, N.J.: Ablex, 1980.

Meade, E. J., Jr. Introduction. In J. J. Marke, *Copyright and intellectual property*. New York: Fund for the Advancement of the Education, 1967.

Meyer, G. TV cassettes – a new frontier for pioneers and pirates. *Bulletin of the Copyright Society of the U.S.A.*, 1971, *29*, 16–47.

Meyers, G. The feat of Houdini or how the new act disentangles the CATV-copyright knot. In New York Law School Law Review, *The complete guide to the new copyright law*. New York: Lorenz Press, 1977. (Originally published, *New York Law School Law Review*, 1977, *22.)*

Miller, J. K. Copyright considerations in teacher- and student-designed learning materials. *Social Education*, 1975, *40*, 282–283.

Miller, J. K. *Applying the new copyright law: A guide for educators and librarians*. Chicago: ALA, 1979.

Miller, J. K. *U.S. copyright documents: An annotated collection for use by educators and librarians*. Littleton, Colo.: Libraries Unlimited, 1981.

Miller, J. K. Issues: What the BOCES decision means. *Instructional Innovator*, September 1982, *27*(6), 37.

Miller, P. C. Copyright: When is fair use not fair? *Educational Technology*, January 1979, *19*(1), 44–47.

Millington, W. G. *The law and the college student: Justice in evolution*. St. Paul, Minn.: West, 1979.

Mills, L. To tape or not to tape. *Teacher*, May–June 1976, *93*(9), 28–29.

Minami, H. Copyright in Japan. In J. S. Lawrence & B. Timberg (Eds.), *Fair use and free inquiry: Copyright law and the new media*. Norwood, N.J.: Ablex, 1980.

Mowrey, R. T. The rise and fall of record piracy. *American Society of Composers, Authors and Publishers Copyright Law Symposium*, 1982, *27*, 155–206.

Munshi, K. S. Mass media and continuing education: An overview. *New Directions for Continuing Education*, 1980, (5), 1–14.

National Commission on New Technological Uses of Copyrighted Works. *Final report of the National Commission on New Technological Uses of Copyrighted Works, July 31, 1978.* Washington, D.C.: Library of Congress, 1979.

Needham, R. Tape recording, photocopying, and fair use. *American Society of Composers, Authors and Publishers Copyright Law Symposium*, 1959, *10*, 75–103.

Nevins, F. M. The new Copyright Act and the classroom use of videotaped films. *Washington University Law Quarterly*, 1978, *1978*, 563–569.

Nimmer, M. B. Foreword: Two copyright crises. *UCLA Law Review*, 1968, *15*, 931–938.

Nimmer, M. B. Does copyright abridge the first amendment guarantees of free speech and press? *UCLA Law Review*, 1970, *17*, 1180–1204.

Nimmer, M. B. Photocopying and record piracy: Of Dred Scott and Alice in Wonderland. *UCLA Law Review*, 1975, *22*, 1052–1065.

Nimmer, M. B. *Cases and materials on copyright and other aspects of law pertaining to literary, musical and artistics work* (2nd ed.). St. Paul, Minn.: West, 1979.

Nimmer, M. B. *Nimmer on copyright: A treatise on the law of literary, musical and artistic property, and the protection of ideas* (4 vols.). New York: Matthew Bender, 1981.

Oakes, J. Copyright and the first amendment. *University of Miami Law Review*, 1978, *33*, 207–246.

Oekonomidis, D. The freedom to quote according to German law. In J. S. Lawrence & B. Timberg (Eds.), *Fair use and free inquiry: Copyright law and the new media.* Norwood, N.J.: Ablex, 1980.

Palmer, S. E. Court delays ruling in videotaping case that concerns educators and librarians. *The Chronicle of Higher Education*, July 13, 1983, p. 13.

Parris, D. The Copyright Revision Act of 1976: An overview. *The Los Angeles Bar Journal*, 1977, *52*, 564–578.

Patterson, L. R. *Copyright in historical perspective.* Nashville: Vanderbilt University Press, 1968.

Patterson, L. R. Copyright and the public interest. In A. Kent & H. Lancour (Eds.), *Copyright: Current viewpoints on history, laws, legislation.* New York: Bowker, 1972. (Originally published, *Encyclopedia of Library and Information Science*, 1972, *6.*).

Patterson, L. R. Private copyright and public communication: Free speech endangered. *Vanderbilt Law Review*, 1975, *28*, 1161–1211.

Peters, M. New copyright law: Developments and issues in the first year of operation. *The Bowker Annual of Library & Book Trade Information* (24th ed.), 1979, pp. 43–46.

Petitioners in "Betamax" case assert that in-home videotaping is "fair use." *Patent, Trademark & Copyright Journal,* 1982, *24,* 453–454.

Photocopying and fair use: An examination of the economic factor in fair use. *Emory Law Journal,* 1977, *26,* 849–884.

Pitt, D. L. Education and the copyright law: Still an open issue. *Fordham Law Review,* 1977, *46,* 91–138.

Project, new technology and the law of copyright: Reprography and computers. *UCLA Law Review,* 1968, *15,* 939–1030.

Publishers file copyright suit against university, faculty, and copy center. *Patent, Trademark & Copyright Journal,* 1982, *25,* 173.

Puffer, M. H. The Supreme Court and copyright liability for retransmission of TV and radio signals: A dubious performance. *American Society of Composers, Authors and Publishers Copyright Law Symposium,* 1981, *26,* 127–149.

Purdy, L. N. The history of television and radio in continuing education. *New Dimensions for Continuing Education,* 1980, No. 5, 15–29.

Ramos, C. R. The *Betamax* case: Accommodating public access and economic incentive in copyright law. *Stanford Law Review,* 1979, *31,* 243–263.

Registrar issues report on library photocoping. *Patent, Trademark & Copyright Journal,* 1983, *25,* 229.

Reiner, R. E. Home videorecording: Fair use or infringment? *Southern California Law Review,* 1979, *52,* 573–634.

Response of the ALA [American Library Association] to the 1982 King Research report on photocopying in libraries. *ALA Washington Newsletter,* 1982, *34*(10), 1–21.

Ringer, B. Copyright law revision: History and prospects. In G. P. Bush (Ed.), *Technology and copyright: Annotated bibliography and source materials.* Mt. Airy, Md.: Lomond Systems, 1972. (Reprinted from *Congressional Record,* June 11–14, 1968, *114.*)

Ringer, B. Copyright in the 1980s. *Bulletin of the Copyright Society of the U.S.A.,* 1976, *23,* 299–310.

Ringer, B. First thoughts on the Copyright Act of 1976. In New York Law School Law Review, *The complete guide to the new copyright law.* New York: Lorenz Press, 1977. (Originally published, *New York Law School Law Review,* 1977, *22.*) (a)

Ringer, B. The unfinished business of copyright revision. *UCLA Law Review,* 1977, *24,* 951–977. (b)

Roberts, M. *Disney/Universal* v. *Sony:* Arguments and conclusions. *The Videocassette & CATV Newsletter,* March 1980, Special Report.

Robinson, S. The Copyright Office: Developments in 1980. *Bowker An-*

nual of Library & Book Trade Information (26th ed.), 1981, pp. 73–78.

Rosenfield, H. N. The constitutional dimension of "fair use" in copyright law. *Notre Dame Lawyer,* 1975, *50,* 790–807.

Rosenfield, H. N. The American constitution, free inquiry, and the law. In J. S. Lawrence & B. Timberg (Eds.), *Fair use and free inquiry: Copyright law and the new media.* Norwood, N.J.: Ablex, 1980

Roth, E. S. Is notice necessary? An analysis of the notice provisions of the copyright law revision. *American Society of Composers, Authors and Publishers Copyright Law Symposium,* 1982, *27,* 245–284.

Ruark, H. C. AV news & reviews. *Technical Photography,* 1983, *15*(5), 42–43.

Saettler, P. *A history of instructional technology.* New York: McGraw-Hill, 1968.

Samuels, E. G. Copyright and the new communications technologies. *New York Law School Law Review,* 1980, *25,* 905–923.

Saunders, J. S. Origin of the "gentlemen's agreement" of 1935. In G. P. Bush (Ed.), *Technology and copyright: Annotated bibliography and source materials.* Mt. Airy, Md.: Lomond Systems, 1972.

Schwartz, T. A. The legal status of video taping of copyrighted materials for educational purposes. *Proceedings of the 45th ASIS Annual Meeting,* 1982, *19,* 268–271.

Scully, M.G. Colleges must obtain licenses to keep videotapes, copyright guidelines say. *The Chronicle of Higher Education,* December 16, 1981, *23*(16), 11–23.

Selected portions of petitioners' brief in *Sony Corp. of America* v. *Universal City Studios,* No. 81–1687. *Patent, Trademark & Copyright Journal,* 1982, *24,* 463–471.

Selected portions of respondents' brief in *Sony Corp. of America* v. *Universal City Studios,* No. 81–1687. *Patent, Trademark & Copyright Journal,* 1982, *25,* 108–122.

Seltzer, L. E. Exemptions and fair use in copyright: The "exclusive rights" tensions in the new copyright act. *Bulletin of the Copyright Society of the U.S.A.,* 1977, *24,* 215–277; 279–337.

Seltzer, L. E. *Exemptions and fair use in copyright, the exclusive rights tensions in the 1976 Copyright Act.* Cambridge: Harvard University Press, 1978.

Shapiro, J. Toward a constitutional theory of expression: The copyright clause, the first amendment, and protection of individual creativity. *University of Miami Law Review,* 1980, *34,* 1043–1075.

Simkin, C. F., & Weinberg, S. M. Fair use under the 1976 Act. In *Infringement of copyrights.* New York: Practising Law Institute, 1981.

Squibb settles suit by eight publishers. *Publishers Weekly,* 1982, *222*(24), 16.

Stedman, J. C. The new copyright law: Photocopying for educational use. *AAUP Bulletin,* February 1977, *63,* 5-16.

Stern, R. H. Software piracy and the copyright laws. *Computer Design,* November 1981, *20*(11), 209-213.

Stewart, S. M. The clearing house system for licenses. *Bulletin of the Copyright Society of the U.S.A,* 1966, *14,* 8-21.

Stork, P. Legal protection for computer programs: A practising attorney's approach. *American Society of Composers, Authors and Publishers Copyright Law Symposium,* 1972, *20,* 112-139.

Strauss, W. The moral right of the author. In the Copyright Society of the U.S.A., *Studies on copyright* (Arthur Fisher Memorial Edition, vol. 2). South Hackensack, N.J.: Fred B. Rothman, 1963. (Reprinted from Copyright Office Study No. 4, 1959.)

Streibich, H. C. The moral right of ownership to intellectual property: Part I – from the beginning to the age of printing. *Memphis State University Law Review,* 1975, *6,* 1-35.

Streibich, H. C. The moral right of ownership to intellectual property: Part II – from the age of printing to the future. *Memphis State University Law Review,* 1976, *7,* 45-84.

Sturdevant, R. I. *Print materials in higher education: Selected issues, resulting changes, "fair use" in the 1976 Copyright Act.* Unpublished doctoral dissertation, University of Southern California, 1980.

Sullivan, P. W. News piracy: An interpretation of the misappropriation doctrine. *Journalism Quarterly,* 1977, *54,* 682-689.

Supreme Court agrees to review Betamax decision. *Patent, Trademark & Copyright Journal,* 1982, *24,* 153-154.

Sword, L. F. Photocopying and copyright law – *Williams & Wilkins Co.* v. *United States*: How unfair can "fair use" be? *Kentucky Law Journal,* 1974-1975, *63,* 256-278.

Symposium – copyrighted and educational media. *Performing Arts Review,* 1977, *7,* 1-90.

Taping and duplication fees. TLC *Guide,* October 15, 1980, *1* (2), 3; 5-6.

Taubman, J. Some implications of copyright to the arts and education. *Performing Arts Review,* 1977, *7,* 296-327.

Timberg, B. New forms of media and the challenge to copyright law. In J. S. Lawrence & B. Timberg (eds.), *Fair use and free inquiry: Copyright law and the new media.* Norwood, N.J.: Ablex, 1980.

Timberg, S. A modernized fair use code for visual, auditory, and audiovisual copyrights: Economic context, legal issues, and the Laocöon shortfall. In J. S. Lawrence & S. Timberg (Eds.), *Fair use and free inquiry: Copyright law and the new media.* Norword, N.J.: Ablex, 1980.

Toffler, A. *The third wave.* New York: Morrow, 1980.

Treece, J. M. Library photocopying. *UCLA Law Review,* 1977, *24,* 1025-1069.

Troost, F. W. Off-the-air videotaping: An issue of growing importance. *Audiovisual Instruction,* June–July 1976, *21*(6), 60–63.

Troost, F. W. The controversy over off-air videotaping. *Phi Delta Kappan,* February 1977, *58,* 463–465.

Troost, F. W. Guidelines for an off-air taping policy for schools. *Educational & Industrial Television,* November 1978, *10*(11), 77–79. (a)

Troost, F. W. The new copyright law and the off-air taping controversy. *CMLEA Journal,* Summer 1978, *1*(3), 24–27.

Troost, F. W. Copyright today: An interesting paradox. *Audiovisual Instruction,* May 1979, *24*(5), 4–5. (a)

Troost, F. W. Copyright today: Current areas of controversy. *Audiovisual Instruction,* December 1979, *24* (9), 52-53. (b)

Troost, F. W. Copyright: Betamax limbo. *Instructional Innovator,* January 1980, *25*(1), 33–34.

Troost, F. W. Personal communication, March 1981.

Troost, F. W. Students – the forgotten people in copyright considerations. *E & ITV,* 1983, *15*(6), 70; 72–74.

Tseng, H. What everyone should know about the copyright law in Wonderland. *Valparaiso University Law Review,* 1977, *12,* 1–24.

Tseng, H. *New copyright U.S.A: A guide for teachers and librarians,* Columbus, Ohio: AMCO International, 1979.

TV taping at home legal. *Los Angeles Times,* January 17, 1984, p. 1.

Tyerman, B. W. The economic rationale for copyright protection for published books: A reply to Professor Breyer. *American Society of Composers, Authors, and Publishers Copyright Law Symposium,* 1974, *21,* 1–34. (Originally published, 18 *UCLA Law Review* 1100 [1971].)

U.S. Congress. *General revision of copyright law.* U.S. Code, Title 17 (1976), 90 Stat. 2541.

U.S. Congress. House. Committee of Conference. *General revision of the copyright law, title 17 of the Unied States Code.* H. Rept. No. 94-1733. 94th Cong., 2d sess., 1976.

U.S. Congress. House. Committee on Patents. *House report 2222, 60th Congress, 2nd session, February 22, 1909, accompanying H.R. 28192, a bill to amend and consolidate the acts respecting copyright.*

U.S. Congress. House. Committee on the Judiciary. *Copyright law revision.* H. Rept. No. 94-1476. 94th Cong., 2d sess., 1976.

U.S. Congress. House. Committee on the Judiciary. *Off-air taping for educational use. Hearings before the Subcommittee on Courts, Civil Liberties, and the Administration of Justice* (96th Cong., 1st sess.). Washington, D.C.: Government Printing Office, 1979.

U.S. Congress. House. Guidelines for off-air taping of copyrighted works for educational use. *Congressional Record,* October 14, 1981, *127*(145), E4750–4752. (97th Cong., 1st sess.)

U.S. Congress. Senate. Committee on the Judiciary. *Copyright law revision.* S. Rept. No. 94-473. 94th Cong., 1st sess., 1975.

U.S. Constitution. Art. I, sec. 8, cl. 8.

U.S. Copyright Office. *General guide to the Copyright Act of 1976.* Washington, D.C.: Government Printing Office, 1977-1978.

U.S. Copyright Office. *Report of the Register of Copyrights – library reproduction of copyrighted works (17 U.S.C. 108).* January 1983. (NTIS No. PB83-148247)

Universal City Studios, Inc. v. Sony Corp.: "Fair use" looks different on videotape. *Virginia Law Review,* 1980, *66,* 1005-1027.

Van Dalen, D. B. *Understanding educational research* (4th ed.). New York: McGraw-Hill, 1979.

Videotaping of copyrighted films by educational group is not "fair use." *Patent, Trademark & Copyright Journal,* 1982, *24,* 257-259.

Wallace, W. The impact of new technology on international copyright and neighboring rights. *Bulletin of the Copyright Society of the U.S.A.,* 1971, *18,* 293-303.

Warren, W. C. Foreword. In B. Kaplan, *An unhurried view of copyright.* New York: Columbia University Press, 1967.

Wasserstrom, A. H. The copyrighting of contributions to composite works: Some attendant problems. *Notre Dame Lawyer,* 1956, *31,* 381-413.

Watson, B. Letter to the editor. *Training,* June 1983, *20*(6), 14.

Weiss, J. Fair use: New off-air recording guidelines. Unpublished Public Broadcasting Service memorandum, January 8, 1982.

Wincor, R. *From ritual to royalties.* New York: Walker, 1962.

WIPO conference decries piracy of copyrighted works. *Patent, Trademark & Copyright Journal,* 1983, *25,* 470.

Words and phrases. St. Paul, Minn.: West, n.d.

Wylie, D. An unconventional look at copyrights. *Audiovisual Instruction,* October 1978, *23*(7), 14-16.

Yankwich, L. R. What is fair use? *The University of Chicago Law Review,* 1954, *22,* 203-215.

Young, J. E. Copyright and the new technologies – the case of library photocopying. *American Society of Composers, Authors and Publishers Copyright Law Symposium,* 1982, *28,* 51-139.

Zemke, R. Training films: What rights do you "buy?" *Training,* April 1983, *20*(4), 7; 10; 13.

Zirkel, P. A. Copyright law in higher education: Individuals, institutions, and innovations. *Journal of College and University Law,* 1975, *2,* 342-354.

Zissu, R. L. Copyright litigation: Infringement and remedies. *Current Developments in Copyright Law,* 1980, pp. 661-721.

COURT CASES

Ager v. *Peninsular and Oriental Steam Navigation Company,* 26 Ch.D. 637 (1884).

Baker v. *Selden,* 101 U.S. 99 (1879).

Berlin v. *E. C. Publications, Inc.,* 219 F. Supp. 911, 138 U.S.P.Q. 298 (S.D.N.Y. 1963), *aff'd,* 329 F.2d 541, 141 U.S.P.Q. 1 (2d Cir. 1964), *cert. denied,* 379 U.S. 822, 143 U.S.P.Q. 464 (1964).

Blumcraft of Pittsburgh v. *Newman Brothers, Inc.,* 159 U.S.P.Q. 167 (S.D. OH 1968).

Bradbury v. *Columbia Broadcasting System,* 174 F. Supp. 733, 123 U.S. P.Q. 10 (S.D. Cal. 1959), *modified,* 287 F.2d 478, 128 U.S.P.Q. 376 (9th Cir. 1961).

Broadway Music Corporation v. *F-R Publishing Corporation,* 31 F. Supp. 817, 45 U.S.P.Q. 309 (S.D.N.Y. 1940).

Bruzzone v. *Miller Brewing Co.,* 202 U.S.P.Q. 809 (N.D. CA 1979).

Cary v. *Kearsley,* 4 Esp. 168, 102 Eng. Rep. 679 (K.B., N.P. 1802).

Chartwell Communications Group v. *Westbrook,* 637 F.2d 459 (6th Cir. 1980).

Classic Film Museum, Inc. v. *Warner Bros., Inc.,* 453 F. Supp. 852, 199 U.S.P.Q. 265 (D. Me. 1978), *aff'd,* 597 F. 2d 13, 202 U.S.P.Q. 467 (1st Cir. 1979).

College Entrance Book Company, Inc. v. *Amsco Book Company, Inc.,* 33 F. Supp. 276, 45 U.S.P.Q. 516 (S.D.N.Y. 1940), *rev'd,* 119 F.2d 874, 49 U.S.P.Q. 517 (2d Cir. 1941).

Columbia Broadcasting Systems v. *Vanderbilt University,* 7336-NA-CV (N.D. Tenn. 1976).

Columbia Pictures v. *National Broadcasting Company,* 137 F. Supp. 348, 107 U.S.P.Q. 344 (S.D. Cal. 1955).

Dallas Cowboys Cheerleaders v. *Scoreboard Posters,* 600 F.2d 1184, 203 U.S.P.Q. 321 (5th Cir. 1979).

Dellar v. *Samuel Goldwyn, Inc.,* 104 F.2d 661, 42 U.S.P.Q. 164 (2d Cir. 1939), *rev'g, Eisman* v. *Samuel Goldwyn, Inc.,* 23 F. Supp. 519, 37 U.S.P.Q. 760 (S.D.N.Y. 1938).

Donaldson v. *Beckett,* 2 Brown 129, 1 Eng. Rep. 837 (H.L. 1774).

Elektra Records Company v. *Gem Electronic Distributors, Inc.,* 360 F. Supp. 821, 179 U.S.P.Q. 617 (E.D.N.Y. 1973).

Elsmere Music v. *National Broadcasting Company,* 206 U.S.P.Q. 913 (S.D.N.Y. 1980), *aff'd per curiam,* 623 F.2d 252 (2d Cir.).

Encyclopaedia Britannica Educational Corporation v. *Crooks,* 447 F. Supp. 243, 197 U.S.P.Q. 280 (W.D.N.Y. 1978), 542 F. Supp. 1156, 214 U.S.P.Q. 697 (W.D.N.Y. 1982), 558 F. Supp. 1247 (W.D.N.Y. 1983).

Folsom v. *Marsh,* 9 F. Cas. 342 (C.C.D. Mass. 1841) (No. 4,901).

Fortnightly Corporation v. *United Artists Television,* 255 F. Supp. 1977, 149 U.S.P.Q. 758 (S.D.N.Y. 1966), *aff'd,* 377 F.2d 872, 153 U.S.P.Q. 696 (2d Cir. 1967), *rev'd,* 392 U.S. 390, 158 U.S.P.Q. 1 (1968).

Fox Film Corporation v. *Doyal,* 286 U.S. 123, 13 U.S.P.Q. 243 (1932).

Franklin Mint Corporation v. *National Wildlife Art Exchange,* 195 U.S.P.Q. 31 (E.D. Pa. 1977), *aff'd* 575 F.2d 62, 197 U.S.P.Q. 721 (3d Cir. 1978), *cert. denied,* 199 U.S.P.Q. 576 (1978).

Goldstein v. *State of California,* 412 U.S. 546, 178 U.S.P.Q. 129 (1973), *rehearing denied,* 414 U.S. 883 (1973).

Henry Holt and Company v. *Liggett and Myers Tobacco Company,* 23 F. Supp. 302, 37 U.S.P.Q. 449 (E.D. Pa. 1938).

Hill v. *Whalen & Martell, Inc.,* 220 F. 359, 18 Copy. Dec. 224 (S.D.N.Y. 1914).

Iowa State University Research Foundation v. *American Broadcasting Companies,* 463 F. Supp. 902, 203 U.S.P.Q. 484 (S.D.N.Y. 1978), *aff'd,* 621 F.2d 57, 207 U.S.P.Q. 97 (2d Cir. 1980).

Italian Book Corporation v. *American Broadcasting Companies,* 458 F. Supp. 65, 200 U.S.P.Q. 312 (S.D.N.Y. 1978).

Karll v. *Curtis Publishing Co.,* 39 F. Supp. 836, 51 U.S.P.Q. 50 (E.D. Wis. 1941).

Kepner-Tregoe, Inc. v. *Carabio,* 203 U.S.P.Q. 124 (E.D. Mich. 1979).

Lawrence v. *Dana,* 15 F. Cas. 26 (C.C.D. Mass 1869) (No. 8, 136).

Leon v. *Pacific Telephone and Telegraph Company,* 91 F.2d 484, 34 U.S.P.Q. 237 (9th Cir. 1937).

Lewis v. *Fullarton,* 2 Beav. 6, 48 Eng. Rep. 1080 (Rolls ct. 1839).

Loew's Inc. v. *Columbia Broadcasting System, Inc.,* 131 F. Supp. 165, 105 U.S.P.Q. 302 (S.D. Cal. 1955), *aff'd sub nom, Benny* v. *Loew's Inc.,* 239 F.2d 532, 112 U.S.P.Q. 11 (9th Cir. 1959), *aff'd per curiam* by an equally divided court, 356 U.S. 43, 116 U.S.P.Q. 479 (1958).

McGraw-Hill v. *Worth Publishers,* 335 F. Supp. 415, 172 U.S.P.Q. 482 (S.D.N.Y. 1971).

Macmillan Co. v. *King,* 223 F. 862 (D. Mass. 1914).

Mathews Conveyer Company v. *Palmer-Bee Company,* 41 F. Supp. 401, 51 U.S.P.Q. 286 (E.D. Mich. 1941), *aff'd,* 135 F.2d 73, 57 U.S.P.Q. 219 (6th Cir. 1943).

Mazer v. *Stein,* 111 F. Supp. 359, 96 U.S.P.Q. 439 (D. Md. 1953), *rev'd,* 204 F.2d 472, 97 U.S.P.Q. 310 (4th Cir. 1953), *aff'd,* 347 U.S. 201, 100 U.S.P.Q. 325 (1954), *rehearing denied,* 347 U.S. 949 (1954).

Meeropol v. *Nizer,* 417 F. Supp. 1201, 191 U.S.P.Q. 346 (S.D.N.Y. 1976), *rev'd in part,* 560 F.2d 1061, 195 U.S.P.Q. 273 (2d Cir. 1977), *cert. denied,* 434 U.S. 1013, 196 U.S.P.Q. 592 (1978).

Meredith Corporation v. *Harper & Row, Publishers,* 378 F. Supp. 686, 182

U.S.P.Q. 609 (S.D.N.Y. 1974), *aff'd,* 500 F.2d 1221, 182 U.S.P.Q. 577 (2d Cir. 1974).

Metro-Goldwyn-Mayer, Inc. v. *Showcase Atlanta Cooperative Productions, Inc.,* 479 F. Supp. 351, 203 U.S.P.Q. 822 (N.D. Ga. 1979).

Millar v. *Taylor,* 4 Burr. 2303, 98 Eng. Rep. 201 (K.B. 1769).

Miller Brewing Company v. *Carling O'Keafe Breweries of Canada,* 452 F. Supp. 429, 199 U.S.P.Q. 470 (W.D.N.Y. 1978).

Mills Music, Inc. v. *State of Arizona,* 187 U.S.P.Q. 22 (D. Ariz. 1975), *aff'd,* 201 U.S.P.Q. 437 (9th Cir. 1979).

Mitchell Brothers Film Group v. *Cinema Adult Theater,* 192 U.S.P.Q. 138 (N.D. Tex. 1976), *rev'd,* 203 U.S.P.Q. 1041 (5th cir. 1979).

Mura v. *Columbia Broadcasting System,* 245 F. Supp. 587, 147 U.S.P.Q. 38 (S.D.N.Y. 1965)

National Subscription Television v. *S & H TV,* 644 F.2d 820 (9th Cir. 1981).

New York Tribune Inc. v. *Otis & Co.,* 39 F. Supp. 67, 49 U.S.P.Q. 361 (S.D.N.Y. 1941).

Nichols v. *Universal Pictures Corporation,* 34 F.2d 145, 2 U.S.P.Q. 139 (S.D.N.Y. 1929), *aff'd,* 45 F.2d 119, 7 U.S.P.Q. 84 (2d Cir. 1930), *cert. denied,* 282 U.S. 902 (1931).

Red Lion Broadcasting Co., Inc. v. *Federal Communications Commission,* 395 U.S. 367 (1969).

The Robert Stigwood Group Limited v. *O'Reilly,* 346 F. Supp. 55, 150 U.S.P.Q. 403 (D. Conn. 1972).

Rosemont Enterprises, Inc. v. *Random House, Inc.,* 256 F. Supp. 55, 150 U.S.P.Q. 367 (S.D.N.Y. 1966), *rev'd,* 366 F.2d 303, 150 U.S.P.Q. 715 (2d Cir. 1966), *cert. denied,* 385 U.S. 1009, 152 U.S.P.Q. 844 (1967).

Rubin v. *Boston Magazine Co.,* 645 F.2d 80, 209 U.S.P.Q. 1073 (1st Cir. 1981).

Sayre v. *Moore,* 1 East. 36ln, 102 Eng. Rep. 139n (K.B. 1785).

Schnapper v. *Foley,* 471 F. Supp. 426, 202 U.S.P.Q. 699 (D.D.C. 1979).

Shapiro, Bernstein & Co., Inc. v. *P. F. Collier & Son Co.,* 26 U.S.P.Q. 40, 20 Copy. Dec. 656 (S.D.N.Y. 1934).

Sheldon v. *Metro-Goldwyn Pictures Corporation,* 7 F. Supp. 837 (S.D.N.Y. 1934), *rev'd,* 81 F.2d 49, 28 U.S.P.Q. 330 (2d Cir. 1936), *cert. denied,* 298 U.S. 669 (1936).

Shipman v. *R.K.O. Radio Pictures, Inc.,* 20 F. Supp. 249, 35 U.S.P.Q. 242 (S.D.N.Y. 1937), *aff'd,* 100 F.2d 533, 40 U.S.P.Q. 211 (2d Cir. 1938).

Sid & Marty Krofft Television Productions v. *McDonald's Corporation,* 562 F.2d 1157, 196 U.S.P.Q. 97 (9th Cir. 1977).

Teleprompter Corporation v. *Columbia Broadcasting System,* 355 F. Supp. 618, 173 U.S.P.Q. 778 (S.D.N.Y. 1972), *modified,* 476 F.2d 338,

177 U.S.P.Q. 225 (2d Cir. 1973), *modified,* 415 U.S. 394, 181 U.S.P.Q. 65 (1974)

Time Incorporated v. *Bernard Geis Associates,* 293 F. Supp. 130, 159 U.S.P.Q. 663 (S.D.N.Y. 1968).

Toksvig v. *Bruce Publishing Company,* 181 F.2d 664, 85 U.S.P.Q. 339 (7th Cir. 1950).

Triangle Publications v. *Knight-Ridder Newspapers,* 445 F. Supp. 875, 198 U.S.P.Q. 28 (S.D. Fla. 1978).

Twentieth Century Music Corporation v. *Aiken,* 356 F. Supp. 271, 177 U.S.P.Q. 751 (W.D. Pa. 1973), *rev'd,* 500 F.2d 127, 182 U.S.P.Q. 388 (3d Cir. 1974), *aff'd,* 422 U.S. 151, 186 U.S.P.Q. 65 (1975).

United States v. *Paramount Pictures,* 66 F. Supp. 323, 69 U.S.P.Q. 573 (S.D.N.Y. 1946), *modified,* 344 U.S. 131, 77 U.S.P.Q. 243 (1948).

United States of America v. *American Trucking Associations,* 310 U.S. 534 (1940).

Universal City Studios, Inc. v. *Sony Corporation of America,* 480 F. Supp. 429, 203 U.S.P.Q. 656 (C.D. Cal. 1979), *rev'd in part, aff'd in part,* 659 F.2d 963, 211 U.S.P.Q. 761, 551 PTCJ D-1 (9th Cir. 1981), *rev'd,* 52 U.S.L.W. 4090 (1984).

Wainwright Securities Inc. v. *Wall Street Transcript Corporation,* 558 F.2d 91, 194 U.S.P.Q. 401 (2d Cir. 1977), *cert. denied,* 434 U.S. 1014, 196 U.S.P.Q. 864 (1978), *aff'g,* 418 F. Supp. 620, 194 U.S.P.Q. 328 (S.D.N.Y. 1978).

Walt Disney Productions v. *Air Pirates,* 345 F. Supp. 108, 174 U.S.P.Q. 463 (N.D. Cal. 1972), *modified,* 581 F.2d 751, 199 U.S.P.Q. 769 (9th Cir. 1978).

Walt Disney Productions v. *Alaska Television Network,* 310 F. Supp. 1073, 164 U.S.P.Q. 211 (1969).

Wheaton v. *Peters,* 33 U.S. (8 Pet.) 591 (1834).

White-Smith Music Publishing Co. v. *Apollo Co.,* 209 U.S. 1 (1908).

Wihtol v. *Crow,* 199 F. Supp. 682, 132 U.S.P.Q. 392 (S.D. Iowa, 1961), *rev'd,* 309 F.2d 777, 135 U.S.P.Q. 385 (8th Cir. 1962).

Wilkins v. *Aiken,* 17 Ves. 422, 34 Eng. Rep. 163 (Ch. 1810).

Williams & Wilkins Company v. *United States,* 172 U.S.P.Q. 670 (Ct. Cl. 1972), 487 F.2d 1345, 180 U.S.P.Q. 49 (Ct. Cl. 1973), *aff'd per curiam* by an equally divided court, 420 U.S. 376, 184 U.S.P.Q. 705 (1975).

INDEX